Colonial Settlements in America

Jamestown
New Amsterdam
Philadelphia
Plymouth
St. Augustine
Santa Fe
Williamsburg
Yerba Buena

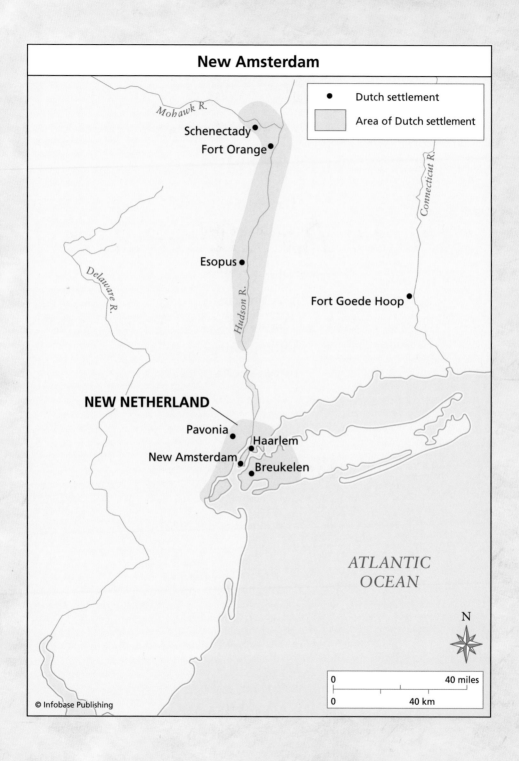

New Amsterdam

- • Dutch settlement
- ▨ Area of Dutch settlement

Mohawk R.

Schenectady •
Fort Orange •

Connecticut R.

Delaware R.

Esopus •

Fort Goede Hoop •

Hudson R.

NEW NETHERLAND

Pavonia •
Haarlem
New Amsterdam •
Breukelen •

ATLANTIC OCEAN

N

| 0 | 40 miles |
| 0 | 40 km |

© Infobase Publishing

COLONIAL SETTLEMENTS
IN AMERICA

New Amsterdam

Tim McNeese

CHELSEA HOUSE
PUBLISHERS
An imprint of Infobase Publishing

Frontis: As displayed on this map of the Dutch colony of New Netherland, the settlement of New Amsterdam was established in the 1620s on the island of Manhattan.

New Amsterdam

Copyright © 2007 by Infobase Publishing

Chelsea House
An imprint of Infobase Publishing
132 West 31st Street
New York, NY 10001

ISBN-10: 0-7910-9334-4   ISBN-13: 978-0-7910-9334-4

Library of Congress Cataloging-in-Publication Data
McNeese, Tim.
  New Amsterdam / Tim McNeese.
     p. cm. — (Colonial settlements in America)
  Includes bibliographical references and index.
  Audience: Grades 7-8.
  ISBN 0-7910-9334-4 (hardcover)
  1. New York (State)—History—Colonial period, ca. 1600–1775—Juvenile literature. 2. New York (State)—History—Colonial period, ca. 1600–1775—Biography—Juvenile literature. 3. Dutch—New York (State)—History—16th century—Juvenile literature. 4. Dutch—New York (State)—History—17th century—Juvenile literature. I. Title.
F122.1.M28 2007
974.7'02—dc22   2006034303

Chelsea House books are available at special discounts when purchased in bulk quantities for businesses, associations, institutions, or sales promotions. Please call our Special Sales Department in New York at (212) 967-8800 or (800) 322-8755.

You can find Chelsea House on the World Wide Web at http://www.chelseahouse.com

Series design by Erika K. Arroyo
Cover design by Ben Peterson

Printed in the United States of America

Bang EJB 10 9 8 7 6 5 4 3 2 1

This book is printed on acid-free paper.

All links and Web addresses were checked and verified to be correct at the time of publication. Because of the dynamic nature of the Web, some addresses and links may have changed since publication and may no longer be valid.

Contents

1

Trade and Strife in the New World

In the warm spring of 1640, an angry group of Raritan warriors ran a party of Dutch traders off the lands the Indians had occupied for, perhaps, hundreds of years. The Dutch had scurried away under "a shower of arrows."[1] It was not the first time these Native Americans living along the Hudson River Valley of modern-day New York had encountered Europeans. For more than a generation, the Dutch had traded with the Native Americans of the region, offering a wide assortment of trade goods dearly sought after by the natives of the Hudson Valley, including axes, knives, mirrors, metal cooking pots, cloth, as well as trinkets, such as glass beads, bells, and buttons. In exchange, the Native Americans had something the Dutch desperately wanted—furs. The pelts of the beaver, fox, and otter were highly prized in Holland and other European markets. Traders who braved the passage from the Old World to the New World loaded their ships with trade items in the hope of earning large profits. The trade relationship worked to the advantage of both the Native Americans and the Europeans. Hides for knives;

skins for axes; pelts for pots—everyone profited according to their wants and needs.

Throughout the early 1600s, then, the Dutch had established several trading outposts along the Hudson River Valley. There were trading centers on Manhattan and Staten Island, along the Connecticut River, on the shores of Long Island Sound, and up the Hudson River at its confluence with the Mohawk River at Fort Nassau, modern-day Albany, New York. The Dutch who manned such outposts were employees of one of the largest trading companies in the world at the time—the Dutch East India Company (also called the United East India Company).

To oversee the business of the fur trade in the North American trading centers, company officials employed a director general, a leader who would be responsible for the company's investments along the Hudson and surrounding region. Often these director generals worked hard to establish good relations with local Native Americans, knowing the company's profits were dependent on cooperation between Dutch traders and the Native Americans. But some leaders did not always understand or remember the delicate relationship that existed between Native Americans and Europeans. After all, with each Dutch settlement or trading post, the Native Americans were expected to give up some of their land. Sometimes, the Dutch tried to force the Native Americans to give into their demands. The year 1640 was one of those times.

The conflict began the previous year, when Governor Willem Kieft of the Dutch West India Company (which had taken control of Dutch interests in North America in 1623) tried to require local Native Americans to pay a "tax" by demanding "contributions" from them of maize, furs, and wampum. (Wampum was the Native American "money." It came in the form of handmade shell beads that were often strung on necklaces or fashioned into elaborate belts.) These demands angered the Native Americans. One group, the Tappan, thought Kieft "must

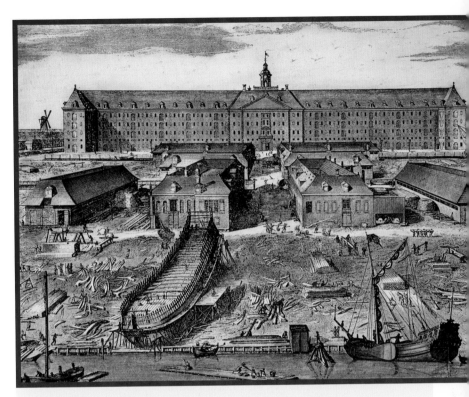

The Dutch East India Company was established in 1602 to carry out trade in Asia, and the first Dutch residents of what would later become New Netherland were employees of this trading company, which was the world's first multinational corporation. Depicted here is a wharf and shipbuilding yard of the Dutch East India Company's facility in Rotterdam, Holland.

be a very mean fellow to come to live in this country without being invited by them, and now wish to compel them to give him their corn for nothing."[2] Their neighbors, the Raritan, had responded by driving the next party of Dutch traders who showed up off their land.

WHERE THE LENAPES DWELL

More than 6,000 years earlier, the ancestors of the Raritans had arrived in the vicinity of the Hudson River Valley. These ancient arrivals lived by hunting small game and foraging for any and all wild edible plants, as well as berries, nuts, and roots. Their diet revolved around such foods as deer, wild turkey, fish, and shellfish. These early Native Americans lived in small groups, perhaps no more than one or two hundred. Finding food for a larger group living in close proximity to one another was difficult otherwise. Around 500 B.C., these prehistoric Native Americans had "discovered the use of the bow and arrow, learned to make pottery, and started to cultivate squash, sunflowers, and possibly tobacco."[3] Another 1,500 years later, they were raising crops of beans and maize. By farming, they were able to support a greater number of people. By the time Columbus reached America in 1492, just five centuries ago, the lands that are today New York City may have been home to approximately 15,000 native people. In addition, perhaps another 50,000 lived in the surrounding lands of modern-day New Jersey, Connecticut, Westchester County, and Long Island.

These tribal groups were different from one another, yet they shared some common cultural traits. Most spoke a dialect of the Delaware language called Munsee. Within the Munsee dialect, the majority used the same word to describe themselves—the Lenape, the "Men" or the "People." They called the lands they occupied, Lenapehoking—"where the Lenapes dwell."[4]

Among the Lenape, there were approximately a dozen bands, or small tribes, scattered throughout the lower Hudson Valley and along other rivers, some serving as tributaries of the great Hudson. There were the Hackensack, along the river of the same name; the Tappan, who called northern New Jersey their home; the Rechgawawanch of Orange County; the Wiechquaesgeck living on the northern end of modern-day Manhattan Island, as well as over in the Bronx; the Siwanoy, whose villages flanked the banks of the East River and the western third of Long Island. Other groups included the Matinecock,

Manhattan, Massapequa, Rockaway, and Merrick. Then, there were the Raritan, whom Europeans found living on today's Staten Island and along Raritan Bay.

These groups of Native Americans valued their individuality; they identified themselves narrowly, giving each a fierce independence from his/her neighbors. They lived in temporary village sites, moving with the seasons. In the spring and early summer months, groups often congregated along seashores, engaging in fishing and gathering clams for food. With the arrival of the fall season, they moved farther inland to gather their crops and hunt the deer that lived in the region in great numbers. When winter threatened, they might move a third time to another village site near a reliable source of firewood and small game, such as squirrels and rabbits. When Europeans arrived, the movements of these Native Americans did not go unnoticed. As one English minister wrote of the Lenape peoples, they lived "very rudely and rovingly, shifting from place to place, accordingly to their exigencies [needs] and gains of fishing and fowling and hunting, never confining their rambling humors to any settled Mansions."[5]

But this freedom to move about with the seasons, to use the land and its resources at their leisure, was interrupted by the arrival of the Europeans during the seventeenth century. The cultural, social, religious, economic, and political differences between the two groups sometimes created hostility. When the Raritans ran off the Dutch traders from their territory in July 1640, Governor Kieft responded. Without even investigating the matter, he sent soldiers to subdue the Raritans in the summer of 1641, resulting in the deaths of several Dutch troops. Some Raritans were also killed, including the brother of a Raritan chief, or sachem, whom the Dutch tortured ". . . with a piece of split wood."[6]

The fighting escalated, with more killings on both sides, leading Kieft to offer "a reward for the head of any one of the Raritans brought to [Fort Amsterdam]."[7]

Soon, other groups of Native Americans joined in the struggle against the Dutch, including the Wiechquaesgeck. During the summer of 1642, a Dutch colonist was murdered by a Hackensack party near Pavonia, across the Hudson River. Later that year, the tribes turned on each other. From the north, a large group of Mahican warriors raided against the Tappan and the Wiechquaesgeck, their traditional enemies who lived above Manhattan. Seventy members of these tribes were killed. In a panic, approximately 1,000 survivors fled south toward the main Dutch settlement, seeking protection.

With this large party of Native Americans encamped nearby, Governor Kieft launched an attack against them on the night of February 25, 1643. A massacre followed with dozens of men, women, and children brutally killed by troops employed by the Dutch West India Company. Excited soldiers returned to their fort on Lower Manhattan, telling tales of babies "torn from their mother's breasts, and hacked to pieces in the presence of the parents, and the pieces thrown into the fire and in the water."[8] Tappans, Wiechquaesgecks, Hackensacks—all were brutally dealt with by the soldiers ordered north by Governor Kieft. When soldiers brought the heads of 80 of their victims into New Amsterdam, Kieft thanked and congratulated them.

WAR ALONG THE HUDSON VALLEY

The massacre only led to a general outbreak of war throughout the region. At least 11 tribal groups of the Lenape, "virtually the entire native population of the lower Hudson Valley,"[9] rampaged through the valley and beyond, taking Dutch victims where they could find them. The angry Native Americans "killed all the men on the farmlands they could surprise" and "burned . . . and destroyed every thing that they could come at."[10]

In 1643, Governor Willem Kieft led a group of troops employed by the Dutch West India Company in an attack against the Native Americans at Pavonia (present-day Jersey City, New Jersey). During the attack, which was the first battle in what would later become known as Kieft's War, Dutch soldiers killed 120 people, including many women and children.

Throughout the small settlement of New Amsterdam, which hugged the southern tip of Manhattan, general panic was the order of the day. Dutch settlers demanded that Governor Kieft do something to stop the attacks. Some blamed him for the ever-expanding conflict. A desperate Kieft met with his council of advisors. They, in turn, sent a dispatch across the Atlantic to company officials in Amsterdam, Holland. The situation was grave.

The salvation for the Dutch came with the arrival of John Underhill, who was sent for from New England, a neighboring colonial region in the hands of the English. Having experience fighting Native Americans in the Pequot War of 1637, Underhill rallied Dutch troops, who relentlessly attacked Indian villages. The slaughter affected the entire region. By the summer of 1645, nearly 1,600 Native Americans and scores of Dutch and English colonists had been killed. Dozens of Native American villages, as well as colonial settlement sites, were destroyed. Kieft's mismanagement had led the Dutch into this deadly war, and he soon lost his position when company officials recalled him before year's end.

Trade between the Native Americans and the Dutch came to an end. The whole reason behind Dutch settlement and the efforts of the West India Company had been compromised. Worried company officials in Amsterdam had a decision to make: Should they try and salvage their efforts in the now-ravaged Hudson River Valley or abandon their colonial efforts altogether? What would the future hold for the Dutch in the region? What would be the fate of New Amsterdam?

2

Early Contacts

The early history of the lands known today as the Americas is shrouded in myth. Sadly, too little is known about the societies created by various culture groups of the earliest residents of the Western Hemisphere—the peoples known today as the American Indians. For hundreds, even thousands of years, the land from modern-day Canada to the southernmost tip of South America was home to thousands of different tribes and family groups who lived off the bounty of an untamed wilderness. It was a land rich in resources. Along the eastern coast of North America, broad quiet streams flowed to the sea. Native Americans fished and swam in these waters. Trees were abundant; thick forests of great oaks, maples, chestnuts, and pine towered over the land, providing the Native Americans with wood for their homes, their canoes, their weapons and tools, sometimes even their clothes. Teeming populations of animals—bears, deer, elk, raccoons, and mountain lions—roamed the wilderness, providing the Native Americans with meat for food and fur for warmth. There were flocks of ducks, geese, and other waterfowl, as well as great schools of fish and seafood—from flounder to lobster, crabs to cod—which were an additional food source for America's first residents. Long before the first Europeans reached the shores of these lands, the American Indians had made these rivers, these meadows, these forests their home.

THE ORIGINAL INHABITANTS OF NEW YORK

Along the northeastern shores of what is today the North American Atlantic Coast, Native Americans called modern-day

---

THE FUR TRADE OF NEW YORK

The explorations and discoveries of such sea captains as Giovanni da Verrazzano and Esteban Gomez did not receive appropriate follow-up by the monarchs who sponsored them during the 1520s. The region of modern-day New York would largely remain unexplored for nearly 90 years. However, Europeans continued to make connections with the Native Americans of this region in another way. They did so, not as sea captains, but as fur traders.

Traditionally, dating back to the Middle Ages, Europeans had always prized animal fur as a luxury item. While the hides or pelts of several animals were commonly sought after, one was highly valued—beaver. Beaver fur was considered important due to its "soft, deep pelt and its alleged medicinal properties."* The oil secreted from the glands of a beaver was used to cure everything from rheumatism to toothaches; poor eyesight to a bellyache.

While the earlier European fur trade was based in Russia, where the city of Kiev served as a market center, discoveries made by early explorers and settlers in North America revealed a world abundant with fur. By the 1580s, the French had established fur trading operations along Canada's St. Lawrence River Valley, north of modern-day New York State. The trade, naturally, included not only European traders and trappers, but American Indians as well; those tribes that had been trapping animals for their fur for hundreds of years. By the turn of the seventeenth century, the fur trade between Europeans and Native Americans along the Eastern seaboard was well established. Another European group, the Dutch, had established trade

New York their home. These Native Americans included the Manhattan tribe. The Manhattans were part of the Delaware tribal group, which was part of a larger group of woodland Indians. Their name—sometimes referred to as *Mana-ha-at* or *Manhattes*—came from an Indian word meaning "island of the hills." Today, with buildings covering the length of New York City's Manhattan Island, these hills are no longer easy to see. But to the Native Americans, the island bounded by two rivers, the Hudson along its west and the East River, was noted for its rocky

connections with the Lenapes of the region by 1598. These Dutch were traders only, not settlers. They came into the region to trade and left when they had accumulated all the furs they could barter for. They did this "without making any fixed settlements, only as a shelter in winter."**

In exchange for furs offered by the Native Americans, the Europeans traded a wide variety of goods. These goods included such items as combs, mirrors, steel knives, tools and iron drills, blankets, bolts of material to make clothing, brass or iron kettles, and lanterns. Such items were highly sought after by many of the Native Americans involved in the trade. These items could be put to use immediately, often replacing old ways of doing things by making them easier. Steel knives meant Native Americans did not have to make their knives out of stone, a slow, tedious process. They would use metal containers to store food, reducing their need for handwoven baskets. European blankets would keep them warm, even as tools and metal hooks helped them farm, hunt, or fish better. While such items might change the lifestyles of these Native Americans on a limited basis, other European trade items had a much greater impact. Two of these were guns and alcohol. In time, Native Americans found themselves dependent on European traders for such items. This resulted in a drastic change to their cultures and an eventual collapse of many of the traditional ways of life.

* Edwin G. Burrows and Mike Wallace, *Gotham: A History of New York City to 1898* (New York: Oxford University Press, 1999), 12.

** Ibid.

The Manhattan tribe resided on present-day Manhattan, the east bank of the Hudson River, and southwestern Westchester County, New York, where their primary village, Nappeckamack, was located. Like most Eastern Woodland Indians, the Manhattans lived in longhouses, which could accommodate as many as 20 families.

hills, which were then covered with woods. Hundreds of years ago, there were other Indian tribal groups on the lands that are today New York City. The Canarsie Indians lived on the land that is today the New York City borough of Brooklyn. To the west, on the opposite banks of the Hudson River, other tribes lived on Staten Island and in New Jersey. These Native Americans sometimes fought one another, as well as other tribes along the Hudson River and others even hundreds of miles away.

Among these various groups, the men were typically hunters, fishermen, and warriors. Meanwhile, the women of these tribes were responsible for much of the work. They built the houses and shelters for their families, raised vegetables in small garden plots, did the cooking and food preservation, and fashioned clothing out of everything from animal skins to tree bark. The world these tribes created for themselves, living off the richness of the American landscape, would continue on generation after generation, with little change. Until, of course, the arrival of new peoples—the Europeans.

THE FIRST EUROPEAN EXPLORERS

The first of the European explorers, a sea captain and mapmaker from the Mediterranean city of Genoa (in present-day Italy), did not reach the shores of modern-day New York. He did not even reach any part of North America. Christopher Columbus, one of the most famous of the early explorers to arrive from Europe, reached lands situated far to the south, in the Caribbean. The year, as every schoolchild knows, was 1492. Although he was from Genoa, Columbus had reached the lands Europeans would soon call the "New World" on behalf of King Ferdinand and Queen Isabella of Spain. (Columbus had sailed west into the forbidding and unknown Atlantic Ocean in an attempt to reach Asia by a direct route. Instead, he had reached lands he mistakenly thought were the Orient.) The Spanish king and queen went to great lengths to follow up on Columbus's first voyage with a second voyage in 1493. Throughout the following century, the Spanish established a series of colonies in the Caribbean, as well as Central and South America. Their efforts to colonize in North America were not quite as successful. In general, the Spanish Empire remained south of the lands that today make up the United States. It would remain for other explorers, those sponsored by the kings and queens of other European countries, to reach and settle the area of the eastern seaboard, where New York is today located.

Like Columbus, one of those explorers was also from Genoa. Little is known about him today. The year of his birth is unknown and even his birth name is unclear. He may have been named Giovanni or Zuan Caboto. History would remember him as the explorer John Cabot. As an adult, Cabot became a celebrated navigator and merchant. He took long-distance trips as far away as Arabia. It was on such trips that Cabot heard stories of the rich spice islands of Asia. In the year 1490, he settled in England along with three sons—Ludovico, Sancto, and Sebastiano. While living there, Cabot added to his reputation as a well-seasoned merchant and skilled seaman. His studies of maps and the stories he heard from other ship captains led this Genoan to formulate ideas similar to those of Columbus. He became convinced that the lands of the Indies (he called them the "isle of Brazil") lay west of the English island, farther north than Columbus believed them to be located.

Once Columbus reached the New World in 1492, Cabot soon heard of his fellow Genoan's voyage and discovery. Cabot believed that Columbus had not reached the Orient, because he had sailed too far south. The talented Genoan gained an audience with the English king, Henry VII, asking him for money and ships to make an exploration to the west himself. By the spring of 1496, just four years after Columbus's first voyage, Henry granted Cabot the right to sail on behalf of England.

Unfortunately, Cabot's first voyage was a disappointment. It ended in failure when a lack of wind and a shortage of supplies forced him to return to England without having made landfall. The following year, he set sail to the west again, this time with the second oldest of his sons, Sebastiano, onboard a single ship, the *Matthew.*

After seven weeks of sailing, Cabot reached the coastline of North America on June 24, 1497. (Cabot was the first European to reach North America in five centuries. The Norsemen of Scandinavia had arrived in the 900s.) It is not known today exactly where Cabot landed. He probably reached the lands of eastern Canada, including Labrador and Newfoundland. Before

Giovanni da Verrazzano was a Florentine explorer who sailed under the employ of France. He is best known for his exploration of the region between present-day Newfoundland and South Carolina in the 1520s, which included a stop at what today is referred to as the Narrows (the strait that separates Staten Island from Brooklyn).

summer's end, he returned to England. His stories of the lands he had explored encouraged King Henry to sponsor another voyage the following year. This voyage involved five ships and 300 men! But Cabot faced additional bad luck. Storms struck his little flotilla of ships on the voyage across, forcing one of his ships to return to England. It would be the only one of Cabot's ships to return. The other four simply disappeared. John Cabot was never heard from again. His previous voyage, however, did give England a claim to the lands of North America that Cabot had discovered. In later years, Cabot's son Sebastiano also sailed to America on behalf of both England (1508) and Spain (1526). Under England's sponsorship, he reached modern-day Hudson Bay in Canada.

ANOTHER SEA CAPTAIN SAILS TO AMERICA

Columbus's "discovery" of the New World had led John Cabot to sail west to make his own discoveries. Other nations sponsored their own explorers, as well, creating an international competition in the search for the Orient and a race to lay claim to American territory. These colonizing powers would include Spain, England, Portugal, and France. The French joined the race in the 1520s. In 1523, King Francis I commissioned yet another Italian seaman, this one from Florence—Giovanni da Verrazzano. (Also sponsoring the voyage was a group of silk merchants from Lyons who wanted a direct connection with the silk trade of China.) Verrazzano was to sail from the Madeira Islands to the Western Hemisphere. Francis was interested in Verrazzano discovering a water route through or around the Americas and continuing on to Asia. This route would become known as the "Northwest Passage." (Such a route does not technically exist. Today, ships can sail north through Arctic waters from the Atlantic to the Pacific, but they have to break up the ice pack as they sail. This was not possible for the ships of the 1500s.)

Verrazzano's fleet included four ships. As had happened to Cabot's ships, storms struck, crippling all but one—*La Dauphine*. This single vessel managed to complete the voyage, reaching North American waters in March 1524, after 50 days at sea. During the following months, Verrazzano explored lands that had already been reached by Cabot, including modern-day Newfoundland. But he sailed much farther south, perhaps as far as the region of South Carolina. His travels did land him along the shores of modern-day New York, which he reached by mid-April. For a while, he plied the waters of Lower New York Bay. His ship sailed through the Narrows to the Upper Bay, a body of water that Verrazzano described as "a very beautiful lake."[11] (Today, the Verrazano Narrows Bridge spans this point of discovery. The bridge was built in 1964. The New York authority that named the bridge chose to change the spelling of Verrazzano's name to Verrazano.) Then, Verrazzano dropped anchor along the southern tip of Manhattan Island at a location that would one day be referred to as the Battery. Here, he traded with the Native Americans. When he and his men ventured out to make contact with the local natives, they were soon surrounded by dozens of Indian canoes, their occupants "clad with feathers of fowls of diverse colors."[12]

The encounter was friendly, but this early meeting between Europeans and American Indians was cut short by a sudden land storm that drove *La Dauphine* out to sea. With that, Verrazzano decided to continue his explorations by heading north. It was a decision that he made with mixed feelings. As he wrote, the lands he had reached—today's cityscape of New York—appeared to be "hospitable and attractive"; a region "not without things of value."[13] Even as he parted, he named New York's Upper Bay "Santa Margarita," after the king's sister.

After further explorations into modern-day New England, where he made contact along Cape Cod with a group of Native Americans known as the Wampanoag, he returned to France and informed the king of all he had seen. However, despite the importance of Verrazzano's discoveries, Francis I did not follow up with future voyages or make any efforts to colonize the region watered by the Hudson and East rivers.

While Verrazzano's visit to the lands that would become New York City would have no long-term impact, Europeans had finally made contact with the Native Americans of the region and had seen the beauty of the bay, its rivers, and the land. The following year, another explorer from Europe reached the same region. He was Esteban Gomez, a black Portuguese sea captain. In early years, he had sailed with the Spanish explorer and seaman Ferdinand Magellan. He reached the mouth of the Hudson River and sailed up the river hoping it might be the Northwest Passage. (He named the body of water Deer River.) His journey up the river was disappointing, because he concluded it was not the route to the East he had hoped to find. Before leaving the area, however, Gomez raided an Indian village in New England and kidnapped 57 Native Americans, taking them back to Lisbon, where they were sold as slaves.

This voyage and raid into the region of modern-day New York and New England would be the last documented landing of a European into those lands for the remainder of the sixteenth century. For more than eight decades, there would be no ships sent by a European monarch to explore the region. There were stories of visits. Several French and English sea captains were rumored to have made landings in the region throughout the second half of the 1500s, but none were documented. One such story told of an Englishman who crossed the Hudson River after walking from the Gulf of Mexico in 1568. There were tales of sailors surviving shipwrecks and washing up on the shores of the Delaware and Hudson rivers during the 1590s and early seventeenth century. Undoubtedly, Spanish and English ships reached the region, if only to raid Indian villages and take slaves for themselves. It would remain for another English explorer, one who sailed to North America on behalf of the Dutch, to expand the legacy of European exploration into the region of New York. It would be from his efforts that the Dutch, in time, established a permanent colony in the north, one they named New Amsterdam. This explorer was Henry Hudson.

3

Henry Hudson's Legacy

The powerful European nation-states—Spain, France, England, and Portugal—flexed their muscles in the New World, establishing colonies from Canada to Brazil during the 1500s. But, by the end of the century and during the early 1600s, smaller, less dominant countries also entered the game of European exploration in the Western Hemisphere. One of those countries was Holland.

A NATION OF REVOLUTION

Prior to 1566, the people of Holland—known as the Dutch— were under the domination of the Spanish Crown. Through much of the 1500s, Spain had developed into a mighty empire in the Americas while also exerting power in Europe. Under the rule of Charles V and his son Philip II, the Spanish had managed to control politics in Portugal; dominate the Holy Roman Empire of the Germanies and the Netherlands (Holland); and conquer the natives of Mexico and Peru, as well as the Philippines. Spain had, indeed, become a global power. Because Spain was a Catholic country, its leaders also tried to squash the new religious movement known as the Protestant Reformation.

But, during the last third of the sixteenth century, Spain's power was being threatened. Despite having gained great wealth from imports of New World gold and silver, the money was starting to run out. Strong naval powers, such as France and especially England, prowled the seas and preyed upon Spanish treasure ships. In Holland, a generalized revolution began to spread. King Philip found himself challenged by the major cities of the Netherlands (or Low Countries, which included modern-day Belgium), such as Antwerp, Bruges, and Brussels. Such trade and merchant towns had grown rich during the end of the 1500s. Fired by Protestantism and wealthy as never before, seven Dutch-speaking provinces of the northern Netherlands, by the 1560s, broke away from Spain and formed the United Provinces, or Dutch Republic (to outsiders, the republic was referred to as "Holland," because it was the largest and richest of the rebellious provinces). Suddenly, the United Provinces, its lands occupying "a mere corner of Europe, not much bigger than the states of Connecticut, Massachusetts, and Rhode Island combined and inhabited by fewer than two million people"[14] was on the road to becoming a European economic powerhouse.

Under the Dutch Republic, the merchants, shippers, and traders of Holland established trade connections from Africa to Russia, and from the Mediterranean to the Spice Islands of the Far East. Dutch trading vessels sailed to the New World, as well, and began establishing settlements in South America and a few of the Caribbean islands. The Dutch were flexing their muscles worldwide. Through the 1570s and 1580s, the Dutch expanded their power and reach. (In 1588, the Dutch had wisely aided the English against a naval invasion launched by King Philip II.) By the 1590s, Dutch seamen had become masters of long-distance navigation, and they were helping establish a colonial empire.

In 1607, the English Muscovy Company employed English navigator Henry Hudson to find a northeastern route to Asia. Both of Hudson's trips were unsuccessful, however, because the route was blocked by the polar ice cap.

Great wealth poured into the Low Countries. Prior to the mid-1580s, Dutch shipping had largely been based on delivering bulk items of no significant value, such as farm products and herring. But increasingly by the end of the 1580s, Dutch ships were engaged in much more lucrative trade. Cargoes included high-profit items, such as pepper, other spices, and sugar. Profits soared.

One of the largest Dutch trading companies formed during this period was the *Vereenigde Oost-Indische Compagnie*, the United East India Company, established in 1602. Based in Amsterdam, it was a giant company, financed by 6 million Dutch guilders, an incredible sum of money at that time. The company's fleet of ships employed no fewer than 5,000 sailors. Primarily involved in the spice trade of the Orient, the company proved to be a formidable rival of other European trading nations in the region, especially Spain and Portugal. But the challenge would not last much longer. By 1609, Holland and Spain called a truce. A weary Spain was no longer able to muster the resources to stand in the way of an ever-expanding Dutch empire.

But the Dutch still found themselves challenged abroad, especially by local Spanish power in the New World. In an attempt to avoid shipping lanes that put Dutch ships in the path of their trade rivals in the Far East, the United East India Company offered a cash prize to any sea captain who could discover a northern route to the Far East. But company officials were interested in a northeasterly passage, not one that flowed north of the Western Hemisphere. An English sea captain named Henry Hudson accepted the challenge. In January 1609, Hudson made contact with East India Company officials. They soon came to an agreement.

HUDSON SETS SAIL

It would be the first time Henry Hudson had made such a voyage. Two years earlier, in 1607, Hudson had sailed in search of a northern route to Asia, not for the Dutch, but for the English Muscovy Company. He had not been searching for the Northwest Passage, but a northeast passage, one that might flow north of Russia. The English captain was certain that he would be able to sail north and east through the Arctic, because he believed it to be ice-free. But he found out otherwise, encountering the 6-million-square-mile Arctic shelf of ice impossible for his 70-foot wooden ship to maneuver through. The trip proved daunting, and Hudson and his crew of 12 were lucky they survived. There were icy, violent storms; illness from rotten bear meat; and a near capsize when a whale tried to surface from under the keel of the ship. Undaunted, Hudson made a second attempt to sail east through frigid waters in 1608, only to find his way blocked by the same immense ice sheet. It would be his last attempt to reach Asia via a northeast route. In his report, Hudson admitted his disappointment with the words: "out of hope to find passage by the North-east."[15] Officials of the English Muscovy Company cut their ties with Hudson.

But, despite these two failures, Hudson was prepared to try yet again. He was now ready to sail on behalf of the Dutch East India Company. He and the company signed a contract on January 8, 1609, with the company promising him a ship by April 1, in time for the 1609 sailing season. He did receive an 85-foot vessel, *Halve Maen* ("*Half Moon*"), manned with a crew of 16, split evenly between English and Dutch sailors. But, once he set sail, reaching Norway and finding ice, Hudson soon steered his ship across the northern Atlantic toward the New World, despite his agreement with the East India Company. He was going to defy company instructions and look for a northwest passage, after all. He talked with his crew about his decision and the possible route they could take to the west. Nearly two weeks later, Hudson and his men set sail for North America.

For three weeks, Hudson's ship sailed west without making landfall or even seeing land. Early in July, tragedy struck when a harsh Arctic storm hit the *Half Moon* and broke off

In 1609, Henry Hudson signed an agreement (depicted in this engraving) with the Dutch East India Company to search for a north-east passage to the Far East. In early April, the company presented Hudson with an 85-foot vessel, the *Half Moon*, and he and his 16-man crew set out less than a week later.

the ship's main mast. This left the ship severely damaged. The *Half Moon* had arrived off Newfoundland and the Grand Banks, where European sailors came each summer to fish in waters thick with cod. Here the men worked on repairing their ship and fished, as well as swam, in the warmer waters of the Gulf Stream. Once they set out again, it was under only one sail. On July 12, Hudson and his men saw modern-day Canada for the first time, probably at Cape Sable, on the south end of Nova Scotia. Here, in Penobscot Bay, the crew spotted two small ships, called *chaloupes*, both French-built, which were in the hands of local Native Americans. (There were several French settlements in the region, because the French explorer Samuel de Champlain had arrived to found a colony in 1603.) Hudson anchored the *Half Moon* within sight of these ships while his crew worked on fitting a new mast to their damaged vessel. A week or so later, the *Half Moon* set out again. But before embarking, some of Hudson's men boarded one of the small French boats and stole it, then raided one of the local Indian villages. With the French chaloupe in tow behind the *Half Moon*, Hudson set a course west of south.

In another week, Hudson again spotted land. Uncertain what land lay before him, Hudson claimed it in the name of Holland. But after a week of exploring and searching for a river opening that might be the Northwest Passage, he realized he had reached Cape Cod, which had already been claimed in 1602 by the English. Hudson sailed on. In another two weeks, his ship reached Smith's Island, which was near the entrance to Chesapeake Bay. The island was named after a friend of Hudson's—Captain John Smith of the Jamestown colony. The English had founded Jamestown, which was only 10 miles farther upriver, just two years earlier. In his journal, Hudson's first mate, Robert Juet, wrote: "This is the entrance into the Kings River in Virginia, where our English-men are."[16] He was in England's colonial backyard, so he sailed a bit farther south to Cape Hatteras Island, then turned around and sailed back north. He poked and prodded at the mouths of other rivers and inlets, including Delaware Bay (he was the first European to reach this body of water), the Susquehanna River, and the South River (Delaware River). But the river that intrigued him the most was one he had learned about from Spanish and French explorations. It was known as the Great River of the North. Hudson set a course for it.

DISCOVERING NEW LANDS

The journey of Henry Hudson into American waters then crossed the path of the site of the future New Amsterdam:

> And so they continued north: misty mornings, bloody sunsets, a stretch of coast like a long smooth cut; surf eternally pounding the belt of sand; while silence beyond. They were aware that they were shouldering a new world, impossibly dark, utterly unknown, of imponderable dimension, and with no clear means of access. And then they felt something happening. Rounding a hooked point, they were startled at what they perceived to be three rivers; cliffs rose up—the land "very pleasant and high, and bold to fall withal." They were in the outer reaches of New York harbor, riding along the coast of Staten Island.[17]

The "three rivers" that Hudson saw before him were Lower Bay, Rockaway Inlet, and one that would be named for him—the Hudson. The captain and his men liked everything they saw before them:

> Vast meadows of grass "as high as a man's middle," forests with towering stands of walnut, cedar, chestnut, maple, and oak. Orchards with apples of incomparable sweetness and pears larger than a fist. Every spring the hills were dyed red with ripening strawberries, and so many birds filled the woods that men can scarcely go through them for the whistling, the noise, and the chattering. Whales, seals, porpoises, twelve-inch oysters and six-foot lobsters crowded offshore waters. Beavers, otters, quail, partridge, pheasants, wild turkeys were too numerous to count. Wild swans, geese, deer, and elk created a hunter's paradise.[18]

Their ship cut a path through waters that teemed with fish, including salmon and mullet. As Robert Juet noted, "The countrey is full of great and tall oake."[19] The harbor, as they discovered, was immense. The day was September 3, 1609.

Hudson and his men anchored the *Half Moon* near modern-day Norton's Point. On September 4, they made contact with local natives who simply appeared out of nowhere. In his journal, Juet described this first encounter: "This day the people of the countrey came aboord of us, seeming very glad of our coming, and brought greene tobacco, and gave us of it for knives and beads. They goe in deere skins loose, well dressed."[20]

Captain Hudson himself wrote of his experience with these Native Americans in his official journal:

When I came on shore, the swarthy natives all stood and sang in their fashion. Their clothing consists of the skins of foxes and other animals, which they dress and make the garments from skins of various sorts. Their food is Turkish wheat [Indian corn, called maize], which they cook by baking, and it is excellent eating. They soon came on board, one after another, in their canoes, which are made of a single piece of wood. Their weapons are bows and arrows, pointed with sharp stones, which they fasten with hard resin. They had no houses, but slept under the blue heavens, some on mats of bulrushes interwoven, and some on the leaves of trees. They always carry with them all their goods, as well as their food and green tobacco, which is strong and good for use.[21]

Nearly 200 years after this encounter between the Delaware Indians (the group called the Lenape) and Henry Hudson and his men, a missionary spoke with the descendents of this group and recorded the story of this important exchange that had been handed down for generations. While the details are unique to the Native American perspective, the general sense that the meeting was "peaceful, wary, curious"[22] is the same. The Delawares of two centuries later described how their ancestors saw "a large house of various colors" skimming along on the water.[23] This confirms the fact that Dutch ships were heavily painted with geometric designs and patterns. The Delaware version tells how the leader of this strange group—Captain Hudson—was wearing a "red coat all glittering with gold lace."[24] This, too, is not without accuracy.

The Native Americans who came down to the water's edge to meet the European strangers were ready to trade. Over the next few days, they presented Hudson and his men with goods for barter. But, while Hudson recorded in his own journal that these Native Americans were "a friendly people," he also noted that they were "much inclined to steal, and are adroit in carrying away whatever they take a fancy to."[25] This led to a violent encounter on September 6, 1609, with a fight ensuing, and one of Hudson's sailors dying from an arrow wound to the neck. But before the melee was over, European guns had killed a dozen or so Native Americans. With that, Hudson decided to leave Norton's Point and press on.

NEW DISCOVERIES, NEW CONTACTS

Over the next several days, Hudson sailed the *Half Moon* through the Narrows between Long and Staten islands (into waters where Verrazzano had sailed three generations earlier). He encountered another group of Native Americans who paddled their canoes out to his ship; they, too, wanting to trade. Cautiously, Hudson bartered with them and purchased "Oysters and Beanes."[26] Then, the English sea captain turned his ship into the mouth of "as fine a river as can be found," one "wide and deep, with good anchoring ground on both sides."[27] It was

In September 1609, Henry Hudson and his crew sailed up the river that would later bear his name—the Hudson. After sailing approximately 150 miles up the river, Hudson determined that he had not found the Northwest Passage and his party headed back south.

the river destined to be called the Hudson. Perhaps this was the elusive passage to the Orient. Hudson thought so, as did his first mate, Juet. It did look promising. As Juet noted of the river's mouth: "The River is a mile broad: there is very high Land on both sides."[28] Throughout the next few days, Hudson managed to sail his ship more than 100 miles up the river. Along the way, the Europeans met other Native Americans, including the Mahicans, who were also friendly to the strangers and offered Hudson and his men a feast of dog meat. Eventually, the *Half Moon* reached the modern-day site of Albany, New York. Although he had high hopes about sailing his ship to the Orient, he came to realize that the Hudson was not the Northwest Passage. There was nothing to do but turn back and head south toward the open sea. Before doing so, Hudson sent a group of sailors on-board the smaller French vessel to scout the region while the others took on casks of fresh water and traded with local Native Americans for food, including much-needed vegetables.

While some of the contacts made by these Europeans went well and were friendly, others were not so amicable. During their return south, another native was caught stealing from the Europeans, near the location of the modern-day city of Pough-keepsie, New York. When another skirmish took place, several Native Americans were killed. The following day, when a war party arrived, the crew boarded the *Half Moon* and responded to this renewed attack by firing a blast from the ship's cannon.

When the reconnaissance group returned to the *Half Moon*, they told Hudson what he was already nearly certain of: that the river channel was becoming too shallow for their ship to continue upriver. In fact, the ship was already in water that was too shallow and soon ran aground, unable to move. Only a rising tide was able to free the *Half Moon*. Hudson sailed south on September 23 and reached the Narrows on October 4, 1609, sailing past "the side of the river called Manna-hata."[29] Soon, he set sail to the east. He had failed to find the Northwest Passage. But he was not entirely disappointed with the results of his voyage. There was an abundance to the land he had "discovered" and a great harbor, where the Dutch might be able to establish trading posts and other settlements. There were furs in the region and Native Americans willing to trade them for European items. When he reached Europe, he did not immediately land in Holland. Instead, he sailed directly to England and landed in Dartmouth after a month at sea.

Why he did not make his first stop in Amsterdam is not clear. Perhaps he was dropping off his English sailors to their homeland. But the decision was a fateful one. He sent a report on to the officials of the Dutch East India Company, and they were not pleased. They ordered him to return to Holland immediately. However, Hudson never again returned to the Netherlands. English authorities were interested in the lands Hudson had explored. Hudson, himself an Englishman,

THE SAD FATE OF HENRY HUDSON

Although Henry Hudson was not allowed to return to Holland, his days of sailing to the New World would not end in 1609. No longer in the employ of the Dutch East India Company, he was soon hired as an agent of the British East India Company, a smaller, but significant trading company of English merchants. They, too, wanted to establish further colonial outposts in the New World. And, like Hudson, they were also interested in finding the Northwest Passage around the north end of the Western Hemisphere. By 1610, they sent Captain Hudson back to North America once again to take up the search for this much-sought-after water route.

Hudson left England on April 17, 1610, onboard a ship named *Discovery* and, almost immediately, ran into trouble. But this time it was not the weather as it had been the previous year. Although the written record is scant, feelings of distrust and disrespect spread through the crew against Hudson. Without question, Hudson could be a vain, arrogant, and extremely fussy leader. His passion for discovering the Northwest Passage probably was stronger than that of his crewmembers, who eventually came to believe Hudson was risking their lives for something that might not even exist.

As Hudson drove his men on, he sailed his ship past Greenland to just south of Baffin Island. Through these waters, the ship was rocked by great ice packs, testing the endurance of the vessel and crew alike. In time, he reached a great open bay that would later be named after him—Hudson Bay. Out in the bay, even Hudson himself was uncertain whether he should continue on. But he waited too long. Unaware he was trapped in the great bay with no way out except the way he had sailed in, the weather closed in on him and his crew, nearly locking them in ice. To save his ship, Hudson ordered it beached on the shore as he and his crew hunkered down for a long winter. The ice remained intact until late in the following spring. By then, the men were finished with Hudson, with many near the brink of starvation. Several crewmembers led a mutiny on June 22, 1611. They placed Hudson, his young son John, and a few other crewmen (those who would not join the mutiny or were too sick to do so) was not allowed to return to Amsterdam. His official papers, charts, and maps, as well as his ship, were seized by the government, and his entire crew dismissed. Hudson was in trouble: "In English eyes English captains were not allowed to work for

In April 1610, Henry Hudson left on what would be his last voyage in search of the Northwest Passage. Hudson's crew mutinied in the spring of 1611 and set Hudson, his son, and seven crewmembers adrift in Hudson Bay.

in a small boat, setting them adrift. They were given some food and a few weapons.

Of the remaining crewmen, only seven managed to make the return trip to England onboard the *Discovery*. By then, they had been reduced to eating "moss, bird bones, sawdust, and candle wax."* Telling their dreadful story to English authorities, they were not punished, even though a mutiny on the high seas was a capital offense under English law. As for Hudson and those set adrift with him, they were never heard from again.

* Donald S. Johnson, *Charting the Sea of Darkness: The Four Voyages of Henry Hudson* (Camden, Me.: International Marine [an imprint of McGraw Hill], 1993), 120.

foreign companies."[30] Eventually, however, Hudson managed to pass his captain's log on to the Dutch East India Company authorities in Amsterdam.

As Dutch officials read Hudson's often glowing words about the lands watered by the river that would be named for him, their interest was piqued. Hudson described the land as "the finest for cultivation that I ever in my life set foot upon."[31] Despite the problems he and his crew had with some tribes, he described the natives along the Hudson River as "a very good people."[32] The great river was wide and deep and good for navigation, Hudson had written. But the words that really jumped off the pages of Hudson's ship log were those that referred to the fur-bearing animals of the region. The land was thick with "many skins and peltries, martins, foxes, and many other commodities."[33] In the years that followed, the Dutch set themselves on a course to establish a colony and tap the natural resources of the North American landscape. At the top of that list of resources was one primary commodity, on which they would found a New World marketplace—fur.

4

Traders Along the Hudson

Despite Henry Hudson's inability to return to Holland fol-lowing his 1609 voyage on behalf of the Dutch East India Company, his trip and his reports had an almost immediate impact on company officials. They remained interested in the search for the Northwest Passage, while at the same time they gained an increased interest in the potential for new markets of trade with American Indians, especially in furs. But others were also interested, including a second group of Dutch merchants. The following year, they hired out some members of the crew of the *Half Moon* to make a return voyage to North America. Exploration was no longer the main objective. Instead, they were to establish more permanent trade relations with the Native Americans. Specifically, their instructions were to sail to the river "called Manhattes from the savage nation that dwells at its mouth."[34] Little is known about this particular ship and crew. Just who were the ship's officers and what was the name of the ship? Its arrival marked the beginning of a long-term Dutch presence in the region that would become modern-day New York. The party did reach modern-day

Manhattan Island, where they built a crude outpost with a few huts, creating a Dutch settlement of sorts. These early Dutch traders laid the groundwork for the future Dutch colony of New Netherland.

TRADING BEGINS

These Dutch merchants found the Native Americans of the region generally open to trade, more so even than they could have hoped for. Because the Dutch brought many exotic items to trade, items that the Native Americans wanted but had no other access to, the trade between the two groups might appear a bit lopsided in favor of the Dutch. It was just as Hudson had written. The Native Americans "were willing to exchange valuable pelts of beaver, mink, and other animals for a cheap knife, an old coat, some gay cloth, and bright buttons and beads, a quick profit could be made by trading."[35]

It was to the advantage of the Dutch that these Native Americans had no interest in money, whether gold or silver. They had their own form of money, or currency, in their wampum beads. The natives labored to grind shells into beads, then strung them into wampum belts or necklaces. Each bead color carried a certain value. White wampum beads were fashioned from the stems of periwinkle shells. Black beads were made from the blue heart of clam shells. Having already established a "bead currency" before the arrival of the Europeans, it should not be surprising that these same natives valued the cheap beads the Dutch offered during trade negotiations.

In time, additional Dutch traders and merchant ships sailed across the Atlantic and docked at New Netherland, taking on cargoes of animal skins. One small merchant ship might return to Holland laden with as many as 7,000 animal pelts from one visit to America.

Then, in 1611, another sea captain came to explore America. He was another Henry (Hendrick in German)—Henry

Henry Hudson's trip to present-day New York convinced the Dutch East India Company to explore the region further and establish trade relations with the local Native Americans. As a result, the Dutch eagerly swapped what they perceived as mundane items for valuable animal furs.

Christiaensen. He was not Dutch, but was born in Cleves, Germany. Christiaensen became the captain of a Dutch ship that sailed to the West Indies to Dutch trading colonies in the Caribbean. On one voyage, he paid a call to New Netherland and the grand harbor that Hudson had "discovered."

Because his vessel was filled with trade goods from the Caribbean, he did not trade much in New Netherland or even attempt to sail up the Hudson River. However, he did make contact with Native Americans to lay the groundwork for future trading trips. After what he had seen of the New World and its opportunities, he decided to take part in the expanding

Hudson River Valley trade. He hired an old friend and sea captain, Adriaen Block, to man his ship. The two men sailed for the New World in a quick trip and, upon their arrival, traded along the Hudson for furs. Christiaensen and Block returned to Holland, taking along two sons of one of the local Indian chiefs who lived along the Hudson River.

CHRISTIAENSEN AND THE *TYGER*

The following year—1612—a group of three wealthy merchants (one was the director of the East India Company) hired Christiaensen and Block to return to America to trade along the Hudson River region. The two captains were each provided a ship—the *Fortune* and the *Tyger*. The two vessels took on cargoes of European trade goods and trinkets for trading with the Native Americans in exchange for valuable furs. The ships reached American waters, and the season of trade was brisk and profitable. The two men decided to return the following year. In fact, Christiaensen made plans to remain on Manhattan Island the following year while Block sailed back to Amsterdam. This would allow Christiaensen to remain in year-round contact with the Native Americans of the Hudson River Valley region.

In 1613, Captain Block made a visit to the region in a small ship called the *Tyger*. Block reached modern-day New York Harbor and landed his ship off the Battery. He made contact once again with the local Native Americans and began a brisk trade, primarily in fur, until he had a shipload. He was determined to return to Holland, having traded successfully in the New World. Then, just as he and his crew were preparing to sail for Amsterdam, a fire broke out on the *Tyger*. As the flames spread out of control, the crew tossed everything overboard they could get their hands on into the ship's boarding boat. Just in time, the sailors abandoned their vessel and managed to escape the flames. As for the *Tyger*, the ship burned down

to the waterline. Block and his men found themselves washed up onshore, having salvaged little more than "a few spare sails, a few tools, and some rope."[36] As for the *Tyger's* valuable cargo of animal pelts, it was lost.

Their accumulated furs destroyed, the Dutch sailors and their captain took an account of their circumstances. Block ordered the construction of adequate shelter. Four huts were soon constructed. They were similar to those used by the Native Americans in the region. Local natives, in fact, helped the stranded Dutch find food. Block was then given command of the traders' second ship, the *Fortune*, which was fitted for passage back to Holland. Block and his sailors were soon on their way back to Amsterdam, leaving in November 1613.

Captain Block had not been gone long before the Dutch traders on Manhattan Island, with Governor Christiaensen as their leader, spotted another ship sailing into the mouth of the Hudson River. It was not a Dutch vessel, however, but an English ship, commanded by Captain Samuel Argall. He had recently been in command of three English warships that had menaced the French to the north in Nova Scotia. His small flotilla had run into a storm, one of the ships had sunk, the second had made a run for open sea, and the third had made its way to the harbor off Manhattan. Not realizing there was a Dutch trading post located there, he chose to force the Dutch to surrender their tiny outpost. With no means of defending himself, Christiaensen had no alternative but to give up the trading colony to the English captain. The Dutch governor signed a letter of submission to the English monarch, King James I, as well as the governor of colonial Virginia. Meanwhile, the letter was delivered to English leaders at the English colony of Jamestown.

Despite this "official" surrender to the English, Governor Christiaensen was not forced to abandon his trading colony.

And he was not prepared to simply walk away. The next time the English came to Manhattan, he would be ready. With the remains of the *Tyger*, he set out to construct "a well-built, sturdy yacht, the first to be constructed on Manhattan Island."[37]

THE RECOVERY OF THE *TYGER*

Early Dutch settlement on Manhattan Island owes much to the exploits and efforts of Governor Henry Christiaensen and Captain Adriaen Block. In the early 1600s, they were two of the first Dutch explorers and traders to begin tapping the lucrative fur markets of the region, sometimes trading little more than trinkets for valuable pelts. In 1613, when Block's ship, the *Tyger*, caught fire and burned to the waterline, it was a dramatic and expensive loss to the Dutch, because the ship was loaded with a season's worth of furs.

While the furs were a total loss, the remaining hull and keel of the *Tyger* were not. Portions of the ship were used to construct a smaller boat, the *Restless*, which Block used to further explore the region along Long Island Sound. Although parts of the *Tyger's* remnants were given a second life, other portions of the ship were simply abandoned, lost to history. That is, until 300 years later.

When the *Tyger* burned, it was floating off the Hudson banks of Manhattan Island. Today, the site would be near the corner of Greenwich and Dey streets (because that spot was filled in with earth over the years), near the former site of the World Trade Center's North Tower. During the early twentieth century, workers for the Interborough Rapid Transit Company (the IRT) were excavating in that area, constructing the city's first modern subway system. Workers for the IRT had uncovered a wide variety of interesting items buried under the earth, including such things as ancient mastodon bones. There were finds that dated back to New York's colonial era, including weapons, tools, household items, and even an occasional chest of coins left behind as buried treasure by some forgotten early citizen of New York.

In 1916, workers uncovered the *Tyger's* prow and keel, as well. It was an extraordinary find, one that sent historians scrambling to identify the historical remains. At the site, subway construction workers sawed off parts of the ship remains and left the rest buried under 20 feet of earth. Those parts are preserved today by the Museum of the City of New York, providing new life for Captain Block's *Tyger*.

The Dutch on the island chopped down trees and fashioned a new keel, cobbling a small craft together as best they could. They pulled the burned-out remains of the *Tyger* out of the water and salvaged additional timbers and some equipment. By the spring of 1614, they had put together a strange-looking boat, which measured only 44½ feet in length by 11½ feet wide. She was dubbed the *Onrust* (the "*Restless*").

NEW WORLD DECISIONS

When Captain Block returned that spring, the two leaders made some important decisions. For one, they chose to move the Dutch trading post to the north away from Manhattan Island and farther up the Hudson River. This would put the Dutch away from the coast, where they had already proved vulnerable to the English. As for Block, he elected to do some important exploring of the region. There was an important incentive to his decision. The government of Holland had announced it would hand off exclusive trading privileges to any company that created the first accurate map of the lands watered by the Lower Hudson and East rivers. With the smaller *Restless* at his disposal, Captain Block had just the right vessel he needed for river exploration. He sailed first up the East River, which is actually a strait. When he floated into the strong channel current that separates the East River from Long Island Sound, he named it *Helle-gatt*, which translates into English as Hell's Gate. Then he sailed up the Connecticut River, followed by an excursion into Narragansett Bay, all the while working on the important map in question. All this exploring would help Captain Block create a useful, accurate, and historically important map:

> The "Figurative Map" that Block brought back to Amsterdam
> later that year was the first to apply the name "Manhates" to

Manhattan, first to show Long Island as an island, first to show the Connecticut River and Narragansett Bay, and the first to use the name "New Netherland" for the lands between English Virginia and French Canada.[38]

Even as Captain Block sailed through the strong waters of Long Island Sound, Governor Christiaensen set about ordering the construction of a new fort. He went up the Hudson River to a location then known as Castle Island. Legend had it that "the Spanish had built a castle-like fort more than fifty years before the Dutch came to build their fort."[39] There, Christiaensen oversaw the building of a moat measuring 18 feet across and surrounding a piece of property 100 feet by 100 feet. Within the moat, the Dutch erected an earthen mound, or breastwork, measuring 4 feet high and between 6 and 12 feet thick. A pair of cannon and 11 smaller swivel guns were mounted on the breastwork. Within the earthen wall, a parade ground was constructed measuring approximately 58 feet square. Here a building was constructed that would provide living quarters for traders, a powder magazine, and storage rooms. When completed, Governor Christiaensen called his new facility Fort Nassau. The governor first stationed a dozen soldiers at the fort. He selected an associate, Jacob Eelkens, to serve as deputy to the governor, his right-hand man. Finished in the summer of 1614, the site served the Dutch in the region for years. Trade resulted in a "great traffick in the skins of beavers, otters, foxes, bears, minks, wild cats, and the like."[40] Today, the location is just south of the state capital of New York, Albany. Another smaller fort also stood on Manhattan Island, which was built the following year.

Almost immediately following the fort's completion, Captain Cornelius Hendricksen, son of Governor Christiaensen, delivered a load of furs onboard the *Fortune* to a rendezvous with Captain Block off the coast of Cape Cod in modern-day

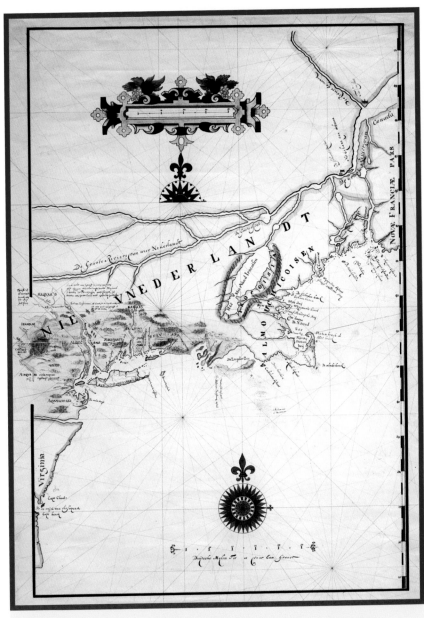

Dutch fur trader and navigator Adriaen Block explored the region between present-day New Jersey and Massachusetts between 1611 and 1614. During his last voyage in 1614, he created this figurative map of the region, which depicted Long Island, the Connecticut River, and Narragansett Bay for the first time.

Massachusetts. There, Block took command of the *Fortune* and once again sailed back to Amsterdam to deliver yet another valuable cargo of pelts. With Block's delivery of furs to Dutch merchants, plus the presentation of his map of the region and the erection of a new trading fort on the upper Hudson River, the Dutch government established a new company to trade with the Native Americans in New Netherland—the United New Netherland Company. (The contract that established the company was the first official government document to use the name "New Netherland.") The contract was signed on October 11, 1614. This company held the exclusive right of trade with Native Americans along the Hudson. Over the next four years, the United New Netherland Company operated Fort Nassau as a year-round post.

Both Captain Block and Governor Christiaensen had played important roles in helping establish a viable Dutch presence along the Hudson River and on the island of Manhattan. Today, a small island at the eastern end of Long Island bears the Dutch captain's name—Block Island. But Christiaensen's role soon came to an end. In 1615, he was killed by a Native American. The reason for the assault is not known. Although Christiaensen would no longer serve New Netherland Colony, it continued on. For the next 50 years, the Dutch would develop their new colony into a thriving and profitable enterprise.

5

New Netherland

With the death of Governor Christiaensen, his deputy, Jacob
Eelkens, soon took the reins of the trading colony as acting governor. It would be a responsibility he would hold unofficially
for the next four years. (No formal appointment was ever made
to replace Christiaensen or to acknowledge Eelkens's leadership.) Even though Christiaensen had been killed by an Indian, Eelkens skillfully led the colony away from taking up arms
against the Native Americans. Trade would continue, and New
Netherland would continue to prosper.

EXPANDING DUTCH TRADE

One important move made by Governor Eelkens was to expand
the trading operations by establishing more Dutch contact
sites with the Native Americans of the region. Trade opportunities had sometimes been lost when a Dutch trader failed to
arrive at an accepted site at a designated time, because the Native Americans would not wait long. The answer seemed to lie
in the erecting of new, permanent trading posts at important

locations. After all, "New Netherland" was an extensive region that included much more than just Manhattan Island. The Dutch claimed lands that include the modern-day states of Rhode Island, Connecticut, western Massachusetts, Vermont, New York, New Jersey, Delaware, and Pennsylvania.

Although Governor Christiaensen had earlier been forced to sign an agreement with the English raider Captain Argall to abandon Manhattan Island, both governors did not honor the agreement. The Manhattan post remained open for business on behalf of Dutch trade. Eelkens did call for the erection of a protective wall around the post. He also kept Fort Nassau up and running. It was an important contact point between Dutch traders and the local Mohawk Indians, as well as other Iroquois tribes, who lived to the west, along the Mohawk River and beyond.

As Eelkens searched for sites for additional trading posts, he sent three Dutch explorers down the Delaware River (it was known as the New River then) in the summer of 1616. These agents sailed into the Catskills, a mountain range in modern-day upstate New York, then south to today's Pennsylvania through the Delaware Water Gap. When they reached the Schuylkill River, near present-day Philadelphia, they were captured by the Minquas Indians. Word was delivered through other tribes of the capture of the Dutchmen. Governor Eelkens sent others onboard the small boat the *Restless* from Manhattan Island south along the New Jersey coast to the Minquas' village. Piloting the *Restless* was Governor Christiaensen's son Cornelius Hendricksen. With offers of trade goods ranging from kettles to beads, the three Dutch captives were freed. Despite this awkward beginning, the Dutch would establish a new trading post on the Delaware River. They would also add posts in present-day New Jersey, Connecticut, and Long Island, in addition to their two older posts: Fort Nassau on the upper Hudson and Fort New Amsterdam on the southern end of Manhattan Island. The Dutch believed they had won the right, through "discovery" and exploration, to claim the territory of North America lying between the Delaware and Connecticut rivers. They had established themselves and had no intention of leaving any time soon.

Trade continued and expanded following 1614 and the rise to power of Governor Eelkens. The United New Netherland Company used its authority under the contract it had been issued in 1614 to trade exclusively with the Native Americans in the Hudson Valley and beyond. But that charter expired late in 1617. By early 1618, the door swung wide open to a "competitive free-for-all" as merchants, traders, and shippers descended on the region, all competing with one another for the same pelts. This competition among Dutchmen in the New World did not seem to serve the sponsoring merchants in Amsterdam very well. By 1621, the Dutch States-General granted authority over New Netherland and the lucrative fur trade to another company. Under this new organization, things were about to change in the Dutch New World colony.

A NEW APPROACH

From the days of Henry Hudson and his explorations along the river that would one day bear his name, Dutch interest in the lands that include modern-day New York were based on the lucrative fur trade. Nearly everyone who came to New Netherland was connected in some way to the brisk business of exchanging animal pelts trapped by Native Americans for European baubles and beads. However, such trade did not create any significant pattern of settlement in the region. There were Dutch men living and working in the trading colony, but there were no women or children to provide social stability.

Then, in 1621, the situation began to change. That year, the Dutch West India Company, a New World alternative to the Dutch East India Company, was established and incorporated. With a peace treaty with the Spanish about to expire, the Dutch

In 1621, Dutch merchants established the Dutch West India Company, which was given jurisdiction over the Caribbean, Brazil, the African slave trade, and North America. Within a year of its founding, Dutch merchants had established settlements and trade warehouses (like the one depicted here) in the Hudson Valley region, including one at what would later become New Amsterdam.

government wanted to have a solid and single trading company in place to meet the potential Spanish challenge. It was a giant company, financed by 7.5 million guilders, the equivalent of tens of millions of dollars today. The West India Company was granted a monopoly over all Dutch trade not only in the Americas, but in Africa, as well. Its purposes were simple—"to make money by trade and to make money by making war on Spain."[41]

Investments in the new Dutch trading company sold quickly. The West India Company rose like a great giant and began to flex its muscles around the globe. By 1623, the Dutch merchant company was prepared to launch its *Groot Desseyn,* its *Grand Design* or *Master Plan.* The company took over several Portuguese sugar plantations in Brazil. The following year, 70 company-sponsored ships preyed on Spanish merchant ships on the high seas, seizing their cargoes. By 1625, more company ships raided and pillaged Spanish settlements in Puerto Rico. Well into the 1630s, the Dutch West India Company hounded the Spanish, with more than 700 ships at its disposal, manned by nearly 70,000 sailors. More than 500 Spanish ships were captured with a total value of 40 million guilders, nearly six times the original investment value of the company in 1621! The Spanish Empire was soon reeling under these pressures, as well as those exerted by England. All told, Dutch efforts cost the Spanish in the 1620s and 1630s as much as 120 million guilders in lost ships and cargoes.

As for the New World and New Netherland, the West India Company maintained its interests there and advanced new settlement. By 1622, within a year of the company's founding, company representatives appeared in the Hudson River region. According to one jealous English account, Dutch agents showed up on "the river Manahata and made plantation there, fortifying themselves in two several places" where "they did persist to plant and trade."[42] Company plans were made to encourage Dutch settlement in the Hudson River region. By November 3, 1623, a new company directive was issued:

> As it is deemed necessary to bring people to Virginius [the name sometimes used to identify New Netherland] it is under consideration to send a ship which will be fitted out by the Chamber of Amsterdam with the necessary trade goods in order to be able to continue the trade as before. The ship will also carry five or six families of colonizers for planting the fields. This ship is available to bring back any remaining goods and people of previous merchants.[43]

Company officials were preparing to get into the settlement business in New Netherland.

In a matter of months following the issuing of the company directive, a ship, the *Nieu Nederlandt* (*New Netherland*), set sail for the Hudson River Valley. It was March 1624. The ship's captain was Cornelis Jacobsz May, who had sailed many times across the Atlantic over the previous decade, so he was no stranger to the Dutch colony in North America. Onboard the ship were 30 families. The majority of them were a group called Walloons, Protestants who had fled from Leyden, a major city in the southern Netherlands. Several members of the immigrant group had earlier petitioned the Dutch government for permission to sail to the English colony of Virginia, but had been refused. According to the contract they signed, these would-be settlers were to establish themselves in New Netherland "near the river of the Sovereign Mauritius."[44] The "Mauritius" was one of the names given the river known today as the Hudson. (Other names at the time included Noord River and Rio de Montagne.)

After setting sail in March, the *Nieu Nederlandt* reached modern-day New York Harbor in early May. The arrival could not have been more fortunate for the Dutch already in the colony. These new colonists found the entrance to the Delaware River blocked by an anchored French ship, its crew ready to drive the Dutch out and claim the region for the French king. The Dutch vessel, "rendered imposing by two cannon"[45] forced the French to leave rather than fight. The way clear, Captain May brought some of the immigrants 144 miles up the Hudson River and docked at Fort Nassau. The fort was in a state of abandon and had to be repaired before it could be used by the new arrivals. Once they had made improvements on the fort, the immigrants renamed it Fort Orange, after the royal family of Holland. The settler-colonists soon began clearing land for farming.

In March 1624, the *Nieu Nederlandt* (*New Netherland*) set sail for the Hudson Valley region with 30 families onboard. The ship reached the Hudson River in May of that year, and some of the immigrants decided to settle at Fort Nassau (present-day Albany), 144 miles from the mouth of the river.

A STREAM OF COLONISTS

Other groups of Dutch settlers soon followed in the wake of this first boatload of immigrants. Families came over and established themselves along the Delaware and Connecticut rivers, on both the eastern and western boundaries of New Netherland. The Dutch fanned out and established themselves in several areas for a good reason.

Over the years, especially following the landing in 1621 of English colonists on the east coast of modern-day Massachusetts (they are remembered today as the Pilgrims), Dutch New Netherland was becoming increasingly surrounded by English colonists. The English settlements in Jamestown and Plymouth placed them both south and northeast of the Dutch colony's centers on Manhattan and at Fort Orange. The English also claimed the region dominated by the Dutch. The settlers who were being delivered to New Netherland were being placed at the mouths of several rivers in the region as "an effort to provide defense against a sea-launched attack, while . . . acquiring control of the water-dependent fur trade that was vital to . . . the colony."[46]

Following the arrival of the *Nieu Nederlandt* in 1624, an expedition of four ships—*Macreel, Paert, Koe,* and *Schaep*—left Amsterdam in April 1625. Onboard was a small herd of cattle, along with five farm organizers, or foremen. There was also a military architect named Cryn Fredericxsz, whose duty it was to organize the building of a new fort on Manhattan Island. The ship also delivered a new director of the West India Company, Willem Verhulst. Captain May had been in charge of the colony of settlers over the past year, but Verhulst now replaced him. When the ships arrived, the cattle were off-loaded on Noten Island (known today as Governors Island), near Manhattan Island. Although the exact date of the arrival of this four-ship flotilla is not known, it is presumed to have been June 1625.

Well-to-do Dutch citizens, such as the couple depicted in this print, had no desire to settle in the New World because they enjoyed a fair amount of freedom in the Netherlands. Consequently, most Dutch settlers in New Netherland were not affluent.

Historians typically mark the beginning of settlement and the founding of New Amsterdam (today's New York City) with the landing of these ships in 1625.

Before sailing from Amsterdam in the spring of 1625, Verhulst had been issued a strict set of instructions from company officials; orders that he was to use in establishing his settlements in the Hudson River region. He was to make certain that there was a church. He was to tolerate no cheating or laziness on the part of his colonists. They were to treat the Native Americans fairly and with kindness, and he was to organize an effort to Christianize the local natives. He was also ordered to steer clear of contact with the English or French as much as was possible. Verhulst was also responsible for planting trees and vineyards in New Amsterdam from the plants and cuttings provided by the company. He was to keep any and all horses out of the hands of the Native Americans. He was also ordered to oversee the construction of a new fortress on Manhattan Island.

The settlers found their new life on Manhattan both difficult and pleasant. Farming was made easier by the good soil on the island. Manhattan was covered with a thick grass "as fine and long as one could wish,"[47] which would provide good grazing pasture for cattle and horses alike. There was an abundance of edible plants and berries on the island, including strawberries growing so thick that the colonists began "to lie down among them to eat them."[48]

DIFFICULT LIVES

The new settlers had to face difficulties as well. Many of these first families who came to New Netherland were extremely poor. The company had paid their ship passage to the New World, as well as many of their other expenses, providing them with livestock, tools, seed, and the land on which to farm. But the land was not deeded to them as their own property. The company continued to own the land. To pay off their debts, the settlers were to work for six years and "to sell everything they raised, over and above what they needed for their own families, to the

THE URBAN PLANNING
OF CRYN FREDERICXSZ

The efforts of the West India Company to establish settlers, including farmers, in New Netherland during the mid-1620s brought much change to the Dutch outpost that had relied for years on fur as the basis of its economy. While the fur trade would continue to be important to the New World, Dutch farming communities, such as New Amsterdam, would gain a new prominence.

As company officials planned for the building of New Amsterdam, they turned to an engineer named Cryn Fredericxsz. Perhaps no one had a greater impact on the design and layout of early New Amsterdam than Fredericxsz. One of his most important assignments was to construct a defensive fortress on Manhattan. He selected a site at the edge of the island, with one side of the fort to face the open water. This would allow those defending the island to see an approaching enemy and launch cannon fire in its direction. Fredericxsz also designed a canal, or moat, to surround the fort. Buildings inside the fort included housing for the governor (or director) of the colony, as well as his clerk and a minister. As Fredericxsz designed the fort, it was to be built in the shape of a pentagon, a five-sided set of walls, raised out of stone.

Fredericxsz was also hired to design several farms for the colony. In the end, he organized five farms for the company, as well as four others, one each for the director, the minister, the clerk, and an assistant clerk. To connect these farms with the village settlement of New Amsterdam, Fredericxsz also designed a set of roads on the island. Today, this early settlement site of New Amsterdam may be found in the part of New York City, where Pearl Street, Broad Street, Beaver Street, Stone Street, and Whitehall Street are located.

While Fredericxsz's efforts did establish much of the design of the New Amsterdam community, he would not remain in the colony for long. Having arrived in 1625, he left the colony to return to the Netherlands by September 1626. He never returned. He left behind a successful colony dotted with buildings, roads, and farms.

As for his fort, it was not completed before he left, and it would remain unfinished for decades. In time, its design was changed from a five-sided structure to a four-square. In fact, the fort was not finished until the governorship of Peter Stuyvesant, who directed New Netherland colony from the 1640s until the 1660s.

company."[49] Colonists were expected to farm and were banned from engaging in the manufacture of any items for distribution and sale—only what they needed to live. Their lives were controlled and restricted. With most Dutchmen being accustomed to a certain amount of freedom back home, they found living in New Netherland restrictive. Meanwhile, back in Holland, few middle-class or wealthy people were tempted to immigrate to America. In their homeland, after all, they lived under a democratic government, had freedom of worship, and could attend school. Nearly anyone who was considered well-off would think twice about coming to America.

But settlers did come. As new farms were being established, Director Verhulst was able to oversee the building of a fort. The engineer, Cryn Fredericxsz, not only oversaw the fort's construction, but other buildings and houses inside and outside the fort, as well as farm buildings, and even roads. He became the "designer of the original town of New Amsterdam and as such he is the building master of present day New York."[50]

But Verhulst's tenure as the leader of the new settlement of New Amsterdam did not last long. He was replaced the following year by another governor—Peter Minuit.

6

Peter Minuit Takes Charge

In Dutch, his name was spelled Pierre Minuyt. American history books typically spell his name Peter Minuit. He arrived on the ship *Meeuwken*, the *Sea Gull*, in New Netherland on May 4, 1626. Minuit was a 46-year-old Walloon whose family roots extended from France to Germany, having been driven out of the latter by the Spanish just a few years earlier. (Growing up, Minuit had spoken German, so Dutch was a second language to him. However, being of French ancestry, his name was pronounced the French way—"Min-wee.") He was to replace the unofficial "governor" of the colony, Willem Verhulst. Minuit had actually visited New Netherland the previous year, in June 1625, along with Verhulst. Verhulst had used him to "investigate the rivers north of Manhattan Island for possibilities of settlements."[51] Verhulst had proven very unpopular with the colonists. He had "bullied the colonists, doctored the books, and managed to lose track of vast quantities of trade goods."[52] Officials of the company had put up with him for

In 1626, Peter Minuit was named the first official director general of the colony of New Netherland by the Dutch West India Company. Later that year, Minuit purchased the island of Manhattan from the Manhattan Indians for $24 worth of trade goods.

less than a year. By 1626, the monopoly granted the West India Company was five years old. The colony had not progressed that much.

BUYING AN ISLAND

There were problems between the Native Americans of the region and the Dutch settlers. The commander of Fort Orange (present-day Albany), Daniel van Crieckenbeek, had recently taken sides in a conflict between the Mahicans and the Mohawks. (He had sided with the Mahicans.) The Mohawks had recently been pushed south by the French living to the north in French Canada. Van Crieckenbeek, accompanied by six of his soldiers, had marched out of Fort Orange along with a Mahican war party. They had traveled no more than three miles from the fort before they were ambushed by Mohawks. Three of van Crieckenbeek's soldiers were killed along with two dozen Mahicans. After the skirmish, the Mohawks drove their point further home "by roasting and eating one especially unfortunate Dutchman named Tymen Bouwensz."[53] This tale of attack and cannibalism spread fear throughout the colony. The company held Verhulst responsible. It was time for him to go. They dispatched Minuit to serve the company and gave him a new title: director general.

When Minuit arrived in New Netherland, he carried instructions from the officials of the West India Company. He was to reestablish security for the Dutch colonists. One of his first tasks was to bring in all the Dutch colonists, who were scattered on farms throughout the Hudson River Valley, and reestablish them in one place for mutual protection. He chose Manhattan Island. There was plenty of land, including good pasturage and farm fields, all surrounded by water. To further secure and make clear their claim over territory previously administered by the old New Netherland Company, Director General Minuit was authorized to "purchase" the island from the local Native Americans. History sometimes tells the story of how Minuit offered the Manhattan Indians on the island $24 worth of trade goods, including beads, trinkets, brightly dyed cloth, blankets, knives, and axes.

(continues on page 68)

DEAL OR NO DEAL?

One of the often-told stories from the early days of European settlement in North America is the tale of Director General Peter Minuit buying Manhattan Island for $24 worth of beads and trade goods from the Manhattan Indians. The purchase is sometimes described as one of the most lopsided land deals in American history, perhaps only second to the American purchase of the Louisiana Territory from the French in 1803 (more than 800,000 square miles) for the equivalent of 4 cents an acre!

But what did this "deal" between the Dutch and the Manhattans really consist of? Did the purchase actually take place? Did the Dutch cheat the Manhattans by paying so little? The story is worth retelling.

There are, in fact, differing versions of the story. Some even give the exact location where the purchase took place. The story really began to become popular during the mid-1800s, with the discovery of a document in Holland, found in the royal archives in 1839. It was a letter written by a Dutch delegate, Peter Schagen, to officials in the Dutch government. The letter is dated November 7, 1626, and describes life in New Amsterdam, including the following passage:

> Yesterday, arrived here the ship *Het Wapen van Amsterdam*, [the *Arms of Amsterdam*] which sailed from New Netherlands, out of the River of Mauritius, [the Hudson River] on the 23rd of September. They report that our people are in good heart and live in peace there; the women also have borne some children there. They have purchased the Island Manhattan from the Indians for the value of 60 guilders; 'tis 11.000 morgens in size [about 22,000 acres].*

These few lines from a long-lost letter are the only documentary evidence of the alleged purchase of Manhattan by the Dutch. The details are scant. Yet the story, as it has been retold over the years, has included all sorts of information beyond the simple reference in Peter Schagen's letter to his bosses in Amsterdam.

The letter does not even mention Peter Minuit as the buyer. However, given the date of the letter and the departure month of the *Arms of Amsterdam*, and that Verhulst never claims to have bought Manhattan, it appears likely that, if such a "purchase" took place, it was made by Minuit.

But the letter does not mention anything about the value of the trade goods in the deal being worth $24. Instead, the amount is 60 guilders. Guilders, of course, are Dutch currency. Although it is not known for certain, it is likely that "someone unknown to historians figured out that sixty guilders

In May 1626, Peter Minuit purchased the island of Manhattan from the Manhattan Indians for 60 guilders ($24) worth of trade goods.

were worth about twenty-four dollars, and the number became part of the story."** Also, the letter does not mention a specific date for the transaction or where exactly it took place, or even the specific trade goods that were swapped for thousands of acres.

Historians do know the types of trade goods that were in common use in the Dutch colony at the time, so assuming certain goods were included is very realistic. It is known that, when Minuit and five other colonists "bought" Staten Island on August 10, 1626, the local Indians there were "paid" with "Some Diffies [duffle cloth], Kittles [kettles], Axes, Hoes, Wampum, Drilling Awls, Jew's Harps, and diverse other wares."*** Assuming Minuit bargained with the Manhattans for trade goods such as cloth, kettles, knives, and axes, the Native Americans would have considered their "deal" with the Dutch to constitute a good trade for them, because they highly prized such items. (Perhaps with the exception of metal kettles. It appears that the Hudson Valley tribes did not like copper kettles much and also did not care for the iron kettles, because they were too heavy to carry around when the tribe moved. The trade goods warehouse at Fort Amsterdam was typically full of trade kettles.)

(continues)

(continued)

But did an actual purchase even take place as far as the Native Americans themselves were concerned? There are no documents to tell the Manhattans' side of the story. Modern-day descendents say no such "purchase" would have taken place. The Manhattans of the 1600s likely agreed to accept gifts from the Dutch in exchange for allowing the colonists, farmers, and traders to use the land, not purchase it. The Manhattans would not have considered land something they had a right to "sell."

The deal of the century, then, may not have been a true deal at all. What is known is that, after the arrival of Peter Minuit, the Dutch West India Company acquired the use of Manhattan from the Native Americans. The island soon became the most important center for the Dutch in the entire colony of New Netherland.

---

* Dirk J. Barreveld, *From Amsterdam to New York: The Founding of New York by the Dutch in July 1625* (San Jose, Calif.: Writers Club Press, 2001), 116.

** L.J. Krizner and Lisa Sita, *Peter Stuyvesant: New Amsterdam and the Origins of New York* (New York: Rosen, 2001), 40.

*** Edwin G. Burrows and Mike Wallace, *Gotham: A History of New York City to 1898* (New York: Oxford University Press, 1999), 24.

(continued from page 65)

Whether the transaction actually took place remains uncertain. But it is certain that Manhattan became the most important part of the Dutch colony of New Amsterdam. With moving more colonists to the island, Minuit organized an effort to have 30 new cabins built on the southern tip of the island before the onset of the winter of 1626–27. A stone trading house with a thatched roof was built nearby, along with a "horsemill," a mill that used a horse for its power, grinding grain into flour. In the top of the mill there was a room that was used for public gatherings and as a church. By year's end, approximately 200 Dutch settlers were calling Manhattan their home.

A STRUGGLING COLONY

Improvements were added slowly to the colony on Manhattan. By 1628, the population of Manhattan was only

270 individuals. These hundreds of Europeans, mostly Dutch citizens, were in the process of transplanting their world to the New World. Many were in the technical employ of the West India Company, but the clock was ticking on most of those arrangements and freedom was assumed after so many years of service. The island of Manhattan was becoming more Dutch every day. As one Dutch physician described this developing colony:

> Men work there as in Holland. One trades, upwards, southwards and northwards; another builds houses, the third farms. Each farmer has his farmstead on the land purchased by the Company, which also owns the cows; but the milk remains to the profit of the farmer; he sells it to those of the people who received their wages for work every week. The houses of the Hollanders now stand outside the fort, but when that is completed, they will all repair [move] within, so as to garrison it and be secure from sudden attack.[54]

Despite all the hustle and bustle of the residents of New Amsterdam, the West India Company found it difficult to make an adequate profit. Company officials spent large sums to bring people to the colony, and it took several years to pay off such amounts and reap profits. During some years, the colony did not earn any profits but instead experienced losses. In 1627, four ships reached New Netherland to take furs back to Amsterdam. None of them returned with a full cargo. The following year, two ships were sent over, but there was no profit. One problem that continued to plague the colony and the company was smuggling. Company employees in the colony were paid small salaries and often had to find supplementary work. Some chose to make money on the side by secretly smuggling furs back to Amsterdam and taking the profits.

THE PATROONSHIP SYSTEM

By 1629, some of the officials in the West India Company decided to try a new plan for the colony. They decided to distribute large tracts of land, measuring thousands of acres, to individuals. These land grants were called patroonships. The individual who received the property was called a patroon. Patroons were supposed to "guarantee that fifty people would go [to his patroonship], not to participate in the fur trade business, but to live on the land and cultivate it."[55] The idea was to grant a virtual monopoly of farming to a few individuals, just as the West India Company held a monopoly to engage in the fur trade along the Hudson River Valley. The patroon did not even have to migrate to the colony himself, but could be an absentee landlord. Patroons would have complete control over their lands, serving as the "lord" of the property, deciding what the rules were and punishing those who broke them. Once implemented, it proved to be an awkward system at best. After all, the ones most anxious to institute this system were three or four investors in the West India Company who wanted to become patroons themselves and make as much money as possible.

One such company official was a wealthy diamond dealer from Amsterdam. His name was Kiliean van Rensselaer. He was granted land on both sides of the Hudson River around Fort Orange, some of the choicest land in New Netherland, totaling 7,000 acres. He called his patroonship Rensselaerwyck. Among the patroonships established along the Hudson River Valley, Rensselaerwyck was the most successful. In fact, it may have been the only one that could be considered a success. Its patroon set out to find his 50 settlers and not only recruited Dutch colonists, but several Norwegians, Swedes, Germans, English, Scotch, and Irish. However, because patroonships centralized all power in such men as van Rensselaer, the company trading

Unlike the settlement of Plymouth, located in what would later become Massachusetts, New Amsterdam struggled to attract colonists. During the first few years of its existence, the settlement grew slowly: by 1628 (around the time of this depiction), the population was just 270.

post at Fort Orange suffered, and trade declined. This was the pattern with most of the patroonships. As the patroons gained more and more power and control over the upper Hudson Valley, Manhattan prospered even more, because there were no patroonships on the island. In time, Manhattan surpassed Fort Orange as the primary Dutch settlement and trading center along the Hudson River.

The timing of the patroonship system ultimately worked against New Netherland Colony as well. When the colony needed to expand and become profitable, the English were busy building a colony of their own nearby, on the coast of eastern Massachusetts. In 1620, even as the West India Company was taking control of the Hudson Valley, a small group of religious immigrants known as Separatists (history often refers to those who arrived onboard their ship, the *Mayflower*, as the Pilgrims) reached the shores of New England. While the Dutch efforts during the 1620s and even the early 1630s failed to produce fruit, the English colony that began at Plymouth and spread to other new settlement sites, such as Boston, prospered and expanded. Throughout the 1630s, the Massachusetts Bay Colony received thousands of new immigrants. They fanned out into new corners of New England and established branch colonies in New Hampshire, Rhode Island, Connecticut, and even the eastern end of Long Island. A new question arose during the 1630s: In the future, which European group would dominate in the Hudson Valley region? Would the Dutch manage to find an alternative to the generally disastrous patroonship system or the heavy-handed control of the West India Company, which was often a disincentive to immigration? Or would the English become the primary trade partner of the Native Americans of the region and their towns the most important settlements of the Northeast? Only time would tell.

7

Incompetent Governors

For six years, Peter Minuit directed the colony of New Nether-land on behalf of the West India Company. His tenure had its bright spots. Between his first year as director (1626) and his last full year (1632), the Dutch fur trade tripled. From this, the company managed to make a small profit. In the end, however, company officials would not be pleased with the profit margin. In addition, the colony continued to deal with many problems. There were not many colonists, and nearly all of them came from the lower class. New Netherland was home to only two "people of substance"[56]: van Rensselaer and Director General Minuit. Because van Rensselaer was not in service to the company, officials could only point to Minuit for blame. He had his critics. A Protestant minister who arrived in the colony in 1628 accused Minuit of being "a slippery man, who under the treacherous mask of honesty is a compound of all inequity and wickedness."[57] In 1630, he fell further out of favor with company officials when he authorized company monies to be spent

After Peter Minuit was relieved of duty as director general
of New Netherland in the early 1630s, Wouter van Twiller
became the new leader of the colony. Upon taking office, van
Twiller attempted to restrict the power of the Dutch West
India Company but was unsuccessful.

on the construction of one of the largest ships built at that
time. But the ship not only proved expensive, it was "clumsy
and hard to handle" in the water.[58] Company officials were
not happy and criticized the project. The first director general
would have to go. He was replaced in 1633 by a 27-year-old

"incompetent man" and "foolish fellow."[59] He was a nephew of
Kiliean van Rensselaer—Wouter van Twiller.

A POOR LEADER

Van Twiller would not prove to be a good director general of New
Netherland Colony. When he tried to purchase land in the Hudson Valley from local Native Americans, they refused. Then, he
quickly antagonized officials of the West India Company when
he made it clear he believed the company's stranglehold on the
economy of the Dutch colony was "stifling the potential of the
colony."[60] When he tried to revoke the company's monopolis-
tic charter over the colony, he failed. There were other failures
on the part of van Twiller. He had a problem with alcoholism.
He was unable to keep colonists from fighting with one another.
Once, during an argument, he ignited a cannon that caused a
fire that burned down a storage shed inside Fort Amsterdam.
Another time he chased a colonist down a New Amsterdam lane
with raised sword in his hand. He was replaced in 1637.

But before he lost his position, van Twiller was able to convince Dutch government officials of the States-General to open
up the colony to immigrants from places other than the Dutch
Republics. Some non-Dutch individuals had already entered the
colony when van Rensselaer recruited his 50 colonists for his patroonship. But the change opened the door wider to colonists
from Europe, including from such countries as England, France,
and Germany, as well as other New World residents from other
colonies, such as New England and Virginia. While this brought
a dramatic increase in New Netherland's population, it reduced
the percentage of colonists who were loyal to Holland.

ANOTHER DIRECTOR GENERAL

As bad as van Twiller had been as New Netherland's leader, his
replacement was even worse. He was Willem Kieft. In a sense, he

fit into the pattern of choices made by the West India Company in selecting director generals. Christiaensen had been Scandinavian, Minuit of French and German descent, and Eelkens was from Normandy. Kieft was from Russian-controlled Kiev, a city located in modern-day Ukraine, where the Dutch had earlier established significant trade connections. (*Kieft* was the Dutch spelling of Kiev.)

As Director General Kieft took over the leadership of the Manhattan outpost, he found himself presiding over a mess,

THE *WILLIAM* INCIDENT

When Peter Minuit was removed from his role as director general over the New Netherland colony, he was replaced by a nephew of Kiliean van Rensselaer, Wouter van Twiller. The appointment proved to be a disaster for the West India Company. While van Twiller failed in his duties in several ways, he did move against a serious challenge when an English ship arrived in the Dutch colony to defy the company's authority and trade with the Native Americans of the Hudson River Valley. The story reveals the difficulties the English were causing the Dutch, including van Twiller.

In the spring of 1633, after some problems with the English in New England, Dutch reinforcements were sent over to protect the colony. They arrived on a ship, the *Soutberch*, which carried 104 soldiers and 52 marines. Technically, Director General van Twiller was their commander. The ship's presence was meant to deter any English who might be tempted to infringe on the Dutch monopoly of trade along the Hudson.

But no sooner had the *Soutberch* docked at Fort Amsterdam than an English ship, the *William*, sailed into the harbor and dropped anchor next to the Dutch vessel. The captain of the English ship was a Dutchman who coolly informed van Twiller he intended to sail up the Hudson and trade with the Native Americans. Van Twiller demanded to see papers from the West India Company authorizing the *William* to enter Dutch waters to trade. The *William's* captain, Jacob Eelkens (who was dismissed by the West India Company in 1628), scoffed at the request and demanded to know where van Twiller's papers were that authorized him to "build settlements in His including company workers trading on their own with the Native Americans, which included selling guns, powder, and shot—all of which were against company rules. There was a general breakdown in discipline in the colony where "drunkenness, theft, fighting, and all forms of immorality flourished; and mutiny and homicides were frequent."[61] Kieft came down hard on the colonists, issuing new policies and rules for those living in New Netherland. To help enforce his new ordinances, Kieft organized a police force of sorts.

Britannic majesty's domain."* This angered van Twiller greatly. He then called his council together, ordered the cannon at Fort Amsterdam trained on the *William*, and then proceeded to get himself drunk.

Captain Eelkens then sailed his ship north up the Hudson. Soon, van Twiller ordered the heavily armed *Soutberch* to pursue the *William*. After missing the incoming tide, the *Soutberch* reached the *William* the following day near Fort Orange. Already, the English ship's crew was busy trading with the Native Americans in the Hudson Valley. Van Twiller ordered his marines ashore. Captain Eelkens was soon arrested, and the *William* confiscated, along with its cargo of recently acquired furs. The *Soutberch* then escorted the English ship to the eastern end of Long Island.

This might have been the end of the incident, except that the English made a formal protest to the Dutch ambassador in London. A heated clash developed between English and Dutch officials until the matter was officially dropped with nothing resolved. Overall, the *William* incident signaled "the beginning of a series of incidents between the Dutch and the English that soured the relation and would eventually bring the two countries on the brink of a colonial war."** This animosity would eventually lead to a showdown between the two powers over who would control the future of New Netherland.

---

* Dirk J. Barreveld, *From Amsterdam to New York: The Founding of New York by the Dutch in July 1625* (San Jose, Calif.: Writers Club Press, 2001),132.

** Ibid., 134.

When Kieft arrived in the colony, New Amsterdam "was a collection of eighty or ninety structures occupied by some 400 or so people, not much bigger . . . than it had been in the days of Pierre Minuyt."[62] There was a row of houses and shops situated along the banks of the East River, where Pearl Street is located today. Approximately one of every four buildings was a grog shop (tavern), where beer and tobacco were sold. After fur, these two items were major sources of income for the West India Company in New Amsterdam.

Kieft set out to make bold changes in New Amsterdam. He worked to redirect life on Manhattan. He banned the sale of alcohol everywhere on Manhattan except for the company store. He began "buying" up land in what are today the New York City boroughs of Queens, Brooklyn, and the Bronx. A booming real estate market developed. In 1641, he established the first annual cattle fair in New Amsterdam. New colonists began to arrive and construction on a stone church began. Kieft tried to address the rivalry between the Dutch and English in the region by forcing all Englishmen in New Amsterdam to swear an oath of allegiance in 1639. The trade town began to return to a new level of prosperity. Kieft appeared to have placed the colony back on its feet. Van Twiller, himself, remained on Manhattan after his directorship and took up farming near Cape Red Hook.

But trouble dogged Kieft's leadership and the colony he directed. In the summer of 1640, Governor Kieft mishandled a conflict with a group of local Native Americans, which resulted in several Dutch and Native American deaths. This led to a general uprising that threatened nearly every settler up and down the Hudson River. Farms were burned by rampaging Native Americans until only three remained on Manhattan and two on Staten Island. The conflict nearly destroyed the Dutch presence in the region, and peace was not restored until August

During his term as director general (1638–1645), Willem Kieft organized the first representative body in New Netherland—the Council of Twelve Men. Kieft is depicted in this woodcut with some of the council members plotting an attack on the Lenape Indians.

1645, when a treaty was signed between the Dutch and several Indian chiefs.

This long-term conflict between European settlers and the Native Americans had devastating effects on New Netherland. It interrupted the flow of immigrants to the colony, just as their numbers had been rising steadily. For years to follow, "hardly anybody was interested to settle down in the Dutch North American colony."[63] The 1640s turned out not to be the best decade for the Dutch in North America, and Kieft proved he was not the right leader. Colonists saw him as arrogant, his reform campaign had petered out, and he was also "a grafter whose cunning and greed made Van Twiller look like a saint."[64] In 1645, Governor Kieft was recalled and replaced by yet another director general of New Amsterdam, one who would last longer than any before him, but one who would eventually be hated by many colonists. His name was Peter Stuyvesant.

After his governorship ended in 1645, Director General Kieft met an untimely end when a ship he was sailing on broke apart in a storm, sending Kieft and more than 80 others to their deaths.

8

"Silver Leg"

After the difficulties raised during Willem Kieft's term as direc-tor general, the West India Company wanted to replace him with someone who would take complete control of New Nether-land and protect the company's interests. Peter Stuyvesant was thought to be that kind of man. He was "able, Loyal, and religious and was a soldier."[65] He had served as a governor before, on the West Indian island of Curacao. He had also provided military leadership. Company officials hoped that Stuyvesant was just the man they needed to direct company business and settlement in New Netherland.

MAKINGS OF A LEADER

In 1645, the year Stuyvesant was appointed director general, he was probably in his late 30s, although the exact year of his birth is unknown. Unlike the director generals before him, he was born in the Netherlands. His parents were strict Protes-tants, members of the Dutch Reformed Church. His father,

The best-known director general of New Netherland was Peter Stuyvesant, who held the position from 1645 to 1664. Stuyvesant was responsible for expanding New Amsterdam beyond the southern tip of Manhattan and building the protective wall around the settlement that later would become Wall Street.

Balthazar Johannes Stuyvesant, was a minister. While religion was an important part of Stuyvesant's upbringing, education was also important. He was a student throughout his younger years, becoming fluent in Latin. By 1630, he attended the University of Franeker. But before year's end, Peter left the university, giving up his studies to become a soldier. It was in the military that he gained many of his organizational skills.

With help from his father, he gained a position with the Dutch West India Company on an island off the coast of Brazil. Drawing the attention of company officials for his dedicated work, he was promoted to another post in Brazil in 1635. Three years later, he was moved to Curacao, the West India Company's headquarters and primary naval base in the Caribbean. By 1642, he was acting governor of Curacao, and neighboring islands Aruba and Bonaire, all part of the Leeward island group off Venezuela. During these years, Stuyvesant oversaw the incoming and outgoing trade at these island outposts. He checked on cargoes entering these Dutch-controlled ports, he gained much practical leadership experience, and his salary was substantial.

In 1644, Governor Stuyvesant's life would change forever thanks to a bold move. That spring, with support from company officials, he led a military and naval campaign against an island held by the Spanish, St. Martin, located 500 miles north of Curacao. This island had important trade items such as salt and tobacco. The Spanish had wrested it away from the Dutch just a few years earlier. Stuyvesant's armada included 12 ships and more than 1,000 soldiers. He had received information that the Spanish position on the island was not very strong. That claim was wrong: the Spanish were extremely strong and well armed. When the Spanish refused to surrender, Stuyvesant's forces laid siege to the island's fort.

As the siege opened, the Dutch invaders built up a low earthen wall outside the fort for their own protection. Having ordered cannon placed on the rampart, Governor Stuyvesant mounted the wall to plant a Dutch flag. From the Spanish fort, a cannon blasted. A Spanish cannonball hurtled through the air.

Stuyvesant was struck, the stone cannonball shattering his right leg. Before he lost consciousness, however, the director general ordered his men to continue their siege. Doctors would have no choice but to amputate Stuyvesant's destroyed limb. Over the following weeks, the siege fell apart, as Stuyvesant could not command the action, suffering "through weeks of delirium following the amputation."[66] When Stuyvesant wrote his report on the campaign to company officials, his words went straight to the point, as he explained how the siege "did not succeed so well as I had hoped, no small impediment having been the loss of my right leg, it being removed by a rough ball."[67] As for his removed limb, doctors fitted Stuyvesant with a wooden leg, bound with silver bands and nails. It was often referred to as his "silver leg." Ultimately, the company rewarded Stuyvesant with a new role—director general of New Netherland. He was to be paid 3,000 guilders annually, "fifty times the purchase price of Manhattan and twenty times the annual wages of a company sailor or seaman."[68]

Between his failed campaign against St. Martin and his arrival in New Amsterdam to assume his duties, Stuyvesant married Judith Bayard, the daughter of a Protestant minister. The new couple left Amsterdam in December 1646 and, after stopping over at Curacao, arrived off Manhattan Island the following August. When he arrived onboard the ship *Princess*, he took a long look at the colony he had been sent to administer. The village was, once again, in dire straits. Stuyvesant took quick stock. The wharf was lined with alehouses. The soldiers who came out to meet the new director general "looked more like ruffians than soldiers."[69] Their uniforms consisted of little more than a leather half-coat, while some wore helmets, others just hats, and some were bareheaded. Stuyvesant had just landed and already he was unhappy with what he saw. Upon seeing the fort itself, Stuyvesant later wrote, "I found [it] resembling more a mole-hill than a fortress, without gates, the walls and bastions trodden underfoot by men and cattle."[70] The new director general immediately began taking charge of the village he called "New Amsterdam." (This was actually a new name for the town. The garrison post had long been called Fort Amsterdam, but the trade village had long been referred to as "Manhattan.") He spoke to a gathered crowd of several hundred curious residents of New Amsterdam waiting to see what their new leader was like. He wasted no time letting them know his intentions: "I shall govern you as a father [does] his children."[71] Before long, the people of this mixed European community were impressed with their new governor.

REMAKING NEW AMSTERDAM

Finding the company town in shambles, Director General Stuyvesant set out to remake the colonial outpost into a disciplined community and urban landscape. He wrote a whole raft of new edicts and decrees, and he would not stop doing so for the next 17 years. He ordered an exact survey of the town to establish accurate property lines. He straightened the streets, which had been a "confounding jumble of lanes and footpaths."[72] In 1658, the residents living along Brouwer (Brewer) Street were allowed to "pave" their street with cobblestones, creating the first of New Amsterdam's stone-surfaced roads, known today as Stone Street. Through the years of his leadership, Stuyvesant could constantly be seen on the streets of the town, moving quickly about despite his wooden leg, issuing new orders. He outlawed pigpens and privies (outhouses) from the town's streets, stating they created "a great stench and therefore great inconvenience to the passers-by."[73] Alehouses were to close at 9 P.M., earlier than before Stuyvesant's arrival, and those who fought in public were harshly punished. He ordered wagoneers to guide their horse wagons through the town to slow down the

flow of traffic. To limit the possibilities of fire, he stopped all
construction of buildings with wooden chimneys and thatched
roofs. He appointed fire wardens to inspect the town's chimneys to make certain they were clean. A police force, called a
"rattle watch," was created in 1658. It included eight officers and
a captain who walked the streets at night to "call out how late it
is, at all corners of the streets from nine O'Clock in the evening
untill the reveille beat in the morning."[74] If any officer found
any suspicious goings-on in the streets, he was to use his rattle
to wake the townspeople.

Believing in the power of religious persuasion, Stuyvesant
had the number of sermons delivered each Sunday increased.
He also demanded that the Sabbath be strictly observed and
that all refrain from trading, social games and interactions, and,
of course, drinking. When he was asked in 1649 and again in
1653 to permit the construction of an orphan asylum, the director general refused, thinking it was the job of good church
deacons and elders to take care of children with no parents.
That same year, New Amsterdam's Reformed Church opened
an almshouse for the old and poor. Monies were collected by
church deacons to pay for the charitable facility. He oversaw the
construction of a hospital in New Amsterdam, the first in the
Dutch company town. Stuyvesant brought change on all fronts
in New Amsterdam. He encouraged a series of public works
projects, focusing on projects to "enhance the town's security,
commerce, or moral order."[75] He had masons brought in to re-
pair the fort. He ordered the local church building to be reno-
vated. A post office was built and opened and a public pier was
built on the East River, near modern-day Moor Street. Workers widened a small creek that ran along today's Broad Street
into a serviceable canal that reminded Dutch residents, along
with the windmills that dotted the tip of Manhattan, of the
world they had left behind in the Netherlands. Such projects,
as well as the many other changes Stuyvesant brought to New

Amsterdam, cost money. Much of it was raised by taxing alcohol in the form of "a reasonable excise and impost on wines, brandy and liquors which are imported from abroad."[76] In time, the changes Stuyvesant brought to his Dutch-sponsored outpost changed New Amsterdam "from a seedy, beleaguered trading post into a well-run Dutch town."[77]

AN EXPANDING COLONY

Under Stuyvesant's leadership, New Amsterdam flourished. By 1655, the non-Indian population of New Netherland was approximately 3,500. Within another 10 years, it had risen to 9,000. Of that latter number, about 1,500 lived in New Amsterdam, "roughly three times as many as Stuyvesant found fifteen years earlier."[78] The population was as diverse as ever. Half were from Germany, England, France, and Scandinavia. By 1665, the Dutch had become a minority in the colony (approximately 40 percent). Approximately one-fifth were Germans and 15 percent were of English descent. This population was different from previous groups of settlers who reached the Hudson Valley in earlier decades. Nearly three out of four came to the colony as families, "couples in their early twenties with small children."[79] While single men had once been a majority in the colony, by the 1660s, they numbered only one in four. Approximately one of every 15 or 16 colonists was a single woman. New Amsterdam, under Stuyvesant, was transformed dramatically:

> Travelers disembarking at the new East River pier in these years would have found themselves near the heart of a bustling, cosmopolitan little seaport. Directly in front of them, facing the river, lay the Strand, a two-block stretch of Paerle Straet [Pearl Street] crowded with taverns, workshops, warehouses, cottages, and brick residences built in the Dutch

Governor Peter Stuyvesant's two-story whitewashed stone house, known as Whitehall, was located on the southern tip of Manhattan. Although the mansion is long gone, the four-block Whitehall Street, between the southern end of Broadway's east fork and the southern end of FDR Drive, is named in its honor.

manner, one or two stories tall, gable-ends out. Just upriver, one block to the right, was the entrance to the Heere Gracht, now lined with houses almost up to what is now Exchange Place. A block to the left stood Stuyvesant's new Great House, a "costly and handsome" two-story residence of white-washed stone—later known as the White Hall [whence the present Whitehall Street]—which boasted extensive gardens and a private dock for the director-general's barge of state. From there it was a short walk across the Marktvelt, past Brugh [Bridge], Brouwers [Brewers, now Stone], and Marktvelt [Marketfield] streets—all densely built up—to the parade-ground [now the site of Bowling Green] at the front gate of Fort Amsterdam. The Heere Wegh [Broadway], which led north from the parade-ground, past the company's garden, was only beginning to attract construction, though. Indeed most of the area beyond the upper end of the Heere Gracht was still occupied by orchards, gardens, and grazing cows.[80]

UNPOPULAR ORDERS

While some of Stuyvesant's changes were undoubtedly good for the growth and prosperity, not to mention the social order, of the New Amsterdam community, his changes and orders had their critics. Sometimes, his moral instructions seemed to go too far for some of the colony's more open-minded, fun-loving residents. Such rules as closing the taverns earlier seemed unrealistic and bothersome. Those convicted of brawling in the streets with knives were punished by serving up to 18 months hard labor on a diet of bread and water. Stuyvesant banned sexual contact between colonists and Native Americans and outlawed liquor sales to Native Americans. He deported prostitutes and outlawed men and women living together "before they have legally been married."[81]

Everyone had to go to church; parties held on boats, carts, or wagons were banned; as was fishing and hunting on Sunday. The first Wednesday of every month was to be a time of fasting and prayer. Stuyvesant, and the city's judges he appointed, created harsher and harsher punishments for those who failed to obey such decrees. In 1660, when a soldier was convicted of a "crime condemned by God,"[82] he was punished by being taken "to the place of execution and there stripped of his arms, his sword to be broken at his feet and he then to be tied in a sack and cast into the river and drowned till dead."[83] A runaway slave was hanged, then his head cut off and placed on a pike in public view. A servant woman who committed arson was ordered "chained to a stake, strangled, and burned."[84] Fortunately for her, the court struck down her punishment before it was carried out.

Although Stuyvesant was a religious man, he had little tolerance for religious practices different from his own. When Lutherans, Quakers, and Jews came to the growing community of New Amsterdam, Stuyvesant saw that ordinances were passed making life difficult for them. Through the years of Stuyvesant's harsh rule, the townspeople became less and less supportive of his leadership.

CHALLENGES FROM ENGLAND

While Stuyvesant proved himself a capable governor of the New Amsterdam community, his service to the colony would finally come to an end. He would not be removed by the company or driven out of town by dissatisfied townspeople. Instead, he was challenged by outside forces—the English. The Dutch along the Hudson Valley had watched anxiously over the years as English colonies were founded and grew in number and population. The English had even claimed the lands occupied by the Dutch on more than one occasion. By 1664, the English monarch, Charles II, decided to push such claims. He granted the land that comprised New Netherland to his brother James II, the Duke of York.

Stuyvesant had anticipated such a move earlier in his governorship. In 1650, he had met with English officials in Hartford, Connecticut (an English settlement in New England), to determine the land rights and borders separating the Dutch colony from those of the English. An agreement had been made called the Treaty of Hartford. But the following year, Holland and England went to war over new laws passed in the

In 1664, the 40-year Dutch reign over New Netherland came to an end when they were forced to cede the colony to the English. Director General Peter Stuyvesant is depicted here among residents who are attempting to convince him to surrender to the English.

English Parliament regarding New World shipping. One such law, the Navigation Act, ordered that European goods delivered to English colonies could only be delivered on English ships or on ships of the country where the goods had been made. This placed a serious restriction on Dutch trade with English colonies. Thus, the two nations went to war.

The war provided an adequate excuse for the takeover of New Netherland by the English. However, attempts made during the 1650s failed. It would not be until the 1660s that the duke of York received permission to take over the Dutch colony. In August 1664, four English warships carrying 2,000 fighting men arrived at the mouth of the Hudson River and

(continues on page 94)

FROM NEW AMSTERDAM TO NEW YORK

Director General Peter Stuyvesant's surrender to the commanders of the English warships that floated menacingly just off Manhattan in the fall of 1664 irrevocably changed the future of those living on the island. It also changed the future of the Dutch West India Company and its investment in North America. Dutch control had come to an end; the new power would be English. But this change did not mean, technically, "a shift from Dutch to English rule but from that of the Dutch West India Company to that of James Stuart, the Duke of York."* Although the duke would have control of a new English colony, it did not signal the end of Dutch influence in the region.

As New Amsterdam came under English control, much of life on Manhattan continued as it had before. Though Stuyvesant had been removed from power, his departure was not mourned by the residents who had come to hate him. But the Dutch colonists were encouraged to remain in New Amsterdam, because their property rights were not taken away, and Dutch culture could continue on in the colony. They could continue to worship in the Dutch Reformed Church in the Dutch language, and their church would continue to collect tithes (taxes) and operate their religious schools. (They would also have to pay to support the Church of England, so they did pay double.) All the Dutch colonists had to do was swear an oath of allegiance to the English monarch, Charles II. They "wouldn't be deprived of their ships, goods, houses, or land, nor would they be compelled to take up arms against [the Dutch provinces] in the future."** What the Dutch had started in the Hudson Valley would continue. Most chose to stay.

The change from Dutch rule to English control went smoothly. For the first year of English dominance over New Amsterdam, the civil officers that had served the Dutch colony, such as schouts, burgomasters, and schepens, continued in their former roles until they were replaced by their English counterparts of mayor, sheriff, and aldermen. Even then, four of the seven elected city aldermen were Dutch.

Over the next century, the Dutch on Manhattan Island hung on to their language. It remained for many of the Dutch residents of New York the language they spoke at home, during worship, and in their schools. However, they also learned English.

Throughout American history and culture, the Dutch continued to have an impact, sometimes in ways that were not even recognized. Three

American presidents were the descendants of Manhattan's original Europeans: Martin Van Buren, and the Roosevelts, Theodore and Franklin. Important nineteenth-century families that would leave their own mark included the Vanderbilts, who became one of the richest families in the United States. Dutch words worked their way into the English language, such as cookie, skipper, sloop, yacht, cole slaw, and waffle. American literature adopted old Dutch tales and ghost stories, such as those of the early nineteenth-century American writer Washington Irving, who became famous for such homely yarns as "Rip Van Winkle" and "The Legend of Sleepy Hollow."

Dutch influences on the modern city that became New York continued over the following centuries. Some of the original street layout is still intact and the original Dutch names—Beaver Street, Stone Street, Pearl Street, Water Street, Broadway, as well as Wall Street—are still used today. Also, New York City's boroughs are part of the original Dutch legacy. The Bronx, Brooklyn, and Harlem were all named by the Dutch. (Brooklyn and Harlem were named for Dutch cities in the Old World.) Brooklyn's Bushwick neighborhood comes from the Dutch word, *Boswijck*, which means "woods district." Another Brooklyn locale, Coney Island, was originally called Conyne Eylandt, "Rabbit Island." Those who live in the New York area can still find themselves visiting other Dutch-named sites such as Hoboken, Stuyvesant Town, Courtlandt Street, Dyckman Street, Vanderbilt Avenue, and others.

Perhaps nothing symbolizes the contribution the Dutch made to the long history of New York more than the city's flag. This emblem features the colors of orange, white, and blue, which were all included in the original Dutch flag that was brought to Manhattan. On the flag is the city's official seal, which includes pictures of a pair of beavers, whose fur had lured Dutch settlement in the first place. Also included are two flour barrels and the four arms of a windmill. Flanking these Dutch symbols are a Manhattan Indian and a sailor representing Dutch ship trade. Nearly 350 years of history have passed since Peter Stuyvesant surrendered Manhattan to the English, but the influence of the people from Holland has never been forgotten.

---

* Edwin G. Burrows and Mike Wallace, *Gotham: A History of New York City to 1898* (New York: Oxford University Press, 1999), 77.
** Ibid.

(continued from page 91)

began positioning themselves around the city, closing it off to the outside world. Hundreds of English troops were off-loaded and spread out across the Dutch countryside. Although Stuyvesant had strengthened the defenses of the town since he took control, the arrival of the English ships signified the end of Dutch rule over Manhattan Island and the surrounding region.

Although Stuyvesant blustered angrily, ready to fight to defend New Amsterdam, he had little to rely on. Fort Amsterdam was in no condition to withstand a siege and its 150 soldiers were short on guns and ammunition. The town did not have enough men to supplement Stuyvesant's inadequate force. And the residents of New Amsterdam, after years of harsh rule by Stuyvesant, were not "willing to risk themselves and their property for him or the West India Company."[85] Stuyvesant had no choice but to surrender. After 40 years of settlement on Manhattan, control of the island passed out of Dutch hands into those of the English.

Chronology

1492 Genoan sea captain and explorer Christopher Columbus sails west across the Atlantic in search of Asia and reaches the Western Hemisphere; his "discovery" spurs European colonization in the New World.

1496–1497 Genoan sea captain John Cabot sails to the New World for England and reaches eastern Canada.

1523–1524 French king Francis I hires Giovanni da Verrazzano, a seaman from Florence, to sail to the New World; he explores along the North Atlantic coast, including the region of modern-day New York (New Netherland).

1560s Seven Dutch-speaking provinces of the northern Netherlands break out from under Spanish control.

1598 Seasonal Dutch traders begin trading with the Lenape Indians on the Hudson River.

1602 The Dutch East India Company is established, a Dutch company designed to rival the Spanish and Portuguese in their overseas trade endeavors.

1607 English sea captain Henry Hudson signs an agreement with the English Muscovy Company to search for a northeast passage to Asia but is unsuccessful.

1608 Hudson makes a second attempt but is blocked by the vast Arctic ice shelf.

1609 Hudson contracts with the Dutch East India Company to search for a northeast passage, but, once at sea, he changes his course for America; he reaches modern-day New York Harbor; on his return to Holland, he is stopped by English authorities who would not let him return to his Dutch employers.

1611–1613 Based on information provided earlier by Hudson, the Dutch launch an effort to establish permanent trading posts along the Hudson River Valley; they send sea captains Henry Christiaensen and Adriaen Block to make contact with the Native Americans in the region.

1614 Governor Christiaensen establishes a trading post up the Hudson River at modern-day Albany, called Fort Nassau; in the meantime, Dutch

Timeline

1598
Dutch traders begin trading with the Lenape Indians on Hudson River

1609
Henry Hudson reaches modern-day New York Harbor

1492
Christopher Columbus sails west across the Atlantic in search of Asia and reaches the Western Hemisphere

1492

1613

1523–1524
Giovanni da Verrazzano explores the region of modern-day New York (New Netherland)

1602
The Dutch East India Company established

1611–1613
Dutch establish permanent trading posts along Hudson River

officials in Amsterdam establish a new company, the United New Netherland Company, which is granted exclusive rights to trade with Native Americans who live in the Hudson Valley.

1615 Governor Christiaensen is killed by a Native American.

1616 New governor of New Netherland, Jacob Eelkens, comes to power.

1617 The United New Netherland Company charter runs out.

1614
Fort Nassau (Albany) established along Hudson River

1624
Dutch West India Company sends colonists to populate New Netherland

1640–1645
Native Americans and Dutch engage in prolonged warfare

1614

1664

1621
Dutch West India Company organized

1626
Peter Minuit becomes governor of New Netherland

1664
English warships force the surrender of the Dutch settlement of New Amsterdam

1621 Dutch States-General organizes a new trading company, the Dutch West India Company.

1622 Representatives of the Dutch West India Company appear in the Hudson River region.

1623 The Dutch merchant company prepares to launch its *Groot Desseyn*, its *Grand Design* or *Master Plan*; it calls for the seizure of Spanish and Portuguese assets around the world, including their American colonies.

1624 The Dutch West India Company sends colonists to populate New Netherland.

1625 Additional shiploads of colonists arrive at the colony on Manhattan Island.

1626 Peter Minuit takes over as governor of New Netherland; before year's end, Minuit "buys" Manhattan Island from the Manhattan Indians.

1629 Dutch company officials create patroon-ship system to encourage colonization to New Amsterdam—it is a failure.

1633 After more than six years of service as governor of New Netherland, Peter Minuit is replaced by Governor Wouter van Twiller.

1637 After four years of poor leadership, van Twiller is replaced by Governor Willem Kieft.

1640–1645 Native Americans and Dutch engage in prolonged warfare throughout the Hudson River Valley.

1645 Governor Kieft is replaced by Peter Stuyvesant, who arrives in New Amsterdam in 1647.

1664 English warships arrive off Manhattan and force the surrender of the Dutch settlement of New Amsterdam; the era of Dutch control and colonization over the Hudson River Valley comes to an end.

Notes

Chapter 1

1. Edwin G. Burrows and Mike Wallace, *Gotham: A History of New York City to 1898* (New York: Oxford University Press, 1999), 38.
2. Ibid.
3. Ibid., 5.
4. Ibid.
5. Ibid., 6.
6. Ibid., 38.
7. Gardell Dano Christensen, *Colonial New York* (Camden, N.J.: Thomas Nelson & Sons, 1969), 53.
8. Burrows and Wallace, 38.
9. Ibid., 39.
10. Ibid.

Chapter 2

11. Ibid., 11.
12. Ibid.
13. Ibid.

Chapter 3

14. Ibid., 16.
15. Russell Shorto, *The Island at the Center of the World* (New York: Vintage Books, 2004), 22.
16. Ibid., 31.
17. Ibid., 32.
18. Dirk J. Barreveld, *From Amsterdam to New York: The Founding of New York by the Dutch in July 1625* (San Jose, Calif.: Writers Club Press, 2001), 80–81.

19. Christensen, 6.
20. Ibid., 15.
21. J. Franklin Jameson, ed., *Narratives of New Netherland, 1609–1664* (New York: Charles Scribner's Sons, 1909), 17.
22. Shorto, 32.
23. Ibid.
24. Ibid.
25. Burrows and Wallace, 14.
26. Ibid.
27. Ibid.
28. Shorto, 33.
29. Ibid.
30. Barreveld, 70.
31. Donald S. Johnson, *Charting the Sea of Darkness: The Four Voyages of Henry Hudson* (Camden, Me.: International Marine [an imprint of McGraw Hill], 1993), 120.
32. Ibid.
33. Shorto, 34.

Chapter 4

34. Burrows and Wallace, 18.
35. Dorothy Niebrugge Hults, *New Amsterdam Days and Ways: The Dutch Settlers of New York* (New York: Harcourt, Brace & World, 1963), 24.
36. Ibid., 26.
37. Christensen, 24.
38. Burrows and Wallace, 19.
39. Christensen, 25.
40. Burrows and Wallace, 19.

Chapter 5

41. Ibid.
42. Ibid., 20.
43. Barreveld, 86.
44. Ibid.
45. William R. Shepherd, *The Story of New Amsterdam* (Port Washington, N.Y.: Kennikat Press, 1926), 9.
46. Barreveld, 87.
47. Shepherd, 9.
48. Ibid.
49. Hults, 30.
50. Barreveld, 111.

Chapter 6

51. Ibid., 112.
52. Burrows and Wallace, 21.
53. Shorto, 47.
54. Burrows and Wallace, 27.
55. Christensen, 42–43.

Chapter 7

56. Barreveld, 130.
57. Ibid.
58. Christensen, 44.
59. Hults, 33.
60. Christensen, 51.

61. Ibid., 53.
62. Barreveld, 139.
63. Ibid., 153.
64. Burrows, 37.

Chapter 8

65. Hults, 47.
66. Shorto, 147.
67. Ibid.
68. Burrows and Wallace, 42.
69. Christensen, 61.
70. Burrows and Wallace, 42.
71. Ibid., 43.
72. Ibid.
73. Ibid.
74. Ibid., 45.
75. Ibid., 46.
76. Ibid.
77. Ibid.
78. Ibid., 50.
79. Ibid.
80. Ibid.
81. Ibid., 58.
82. Ibid.
83. Ibid., 59.
84. Ibid.
85. Ibid., 73.

Bibliography

Barreveld, Dirk J. *From Amsterdam to New York: The Founding of New York by the Dutch in July 1625*. San Jose, Calif.: Writers Club Press, 2001.

Burrows, Edwin G., and Mike Wallace. *Gotham: A History of New York City to 1898*. New York: Oxford University Press, 1999.

Carmer, Carl. *The Hudson*. New York: Farrar & Rinehart, 1939.

Christensen, Gardell Dano. *Colonial New York*. Camden, N.J.: Thomas Nelson & Sons, 1969.

Goodwin, Maud Wilder. *Dutch and English on the Hudson: A Chronicle of Colonial New York*. New York: United States Publishers Association, 1919.

Hults, Dorothy Niebrugge. *New Amsterdam Days and Ways: The Dutch Settlers of New York*. New York: Harcourt, Brace & World, 1963.

Johnson, Donald S. *Charting the Sea of Darkness: The Four Voyages of Henry Hudson*. Camden, Me.: International Marine (an imprint of McGraw Hill), 1993.

McNeese, Tim. *The Hudson River*. Philadelphia: Chelsea House Publishers, 2004.

Nutting, Wallace. *New York Beautiful*. New York: Bonanza Books, 1927.

Shepherd, William R. *The Story of New Amsterdam*. Port Washington, N.Y.: Kennikat Press, 1926.

Shorto, Russell. *The Island at the Center of the World*. New York: Vintage Books, 2004.

Watson, Virginia. *The Trail of Courage: A Story of New Amsterdam*. New York: Coward-McCann, 1948.

Further Reading

Banks, Joan. *Peter Stuyvesant: Dutch Military Leader*. Philadelphia: Chelsea House Publishers, 2000.

Crouse, Anna and Russel. *Peter Stuyvesant of Old New York*. New York: Random House, 1954.

Emerson, Caroline D. *New Amsterdam: Old Holland in the New World*. Champaign, Ill.: Garrard, 1967.

Fischer, Laura. *Life in New Amsterdam*. Chicago: Heinemann Library, 2003.

Krizner, L. J., and Lisa Sita. *Peter Stuyvesant: New Amsterdam and the Origins of New York*. New York: Rosen, 2001.

Spier, Peter. *The Legend of New Amsterdam*. Garden City, N.Y.: Doubleday & Company, 1979.

Web sites

History of New Netherland
www.coins.nd.edu/ColCoin/ColCoinIntros/NNHistory.html

Dutch Colonies
www.cr.nps.gov/nr/travel/kingston/colonization.htm

The Half Moon
www.halfmoon.mus.ny.us/livinghistory.htm

History of Holland
www.historyofholland.com/peter-minuit.html

New Netherland Virtual Tour
www.nnp.org/newvtour/index.html

The New Netherland Dutch
www.nysm.nysed.gov/albany/nnd.html

Information on Governor Peter Stuyvesant
www.peterstuyvesant.org

New Netherland
www.threerivershms.com/dbpsnewnetherland.htm

The New Netherland
www.u-s-history.com/pages/h561.html

Picture Credits

Index

About the Author

Series editor and author **TIM MCNEESE** is associate professor of history at York College in York, Nebraska, where he is in his fifteenth year of college instruction. Professor McNeese earned an Associate of Arts degree from York College, a Bachelor of Arts in history and political science from Harding University, and a Master of Arts in history from Missouri State University. A prolific author of books for elementary, middle, high school, and college readers, McNeese has published more than 80 books and educational materials over the past 20 years, on everything from Picasso to landmark Supreme Court decisions. His writing has earned him a citation in the library reference work *Contemporary Authors*. In 2006, McNeese appeared on the History Channel program *Risk Takers/History Makers: John Wesley Powell and the Grand Canyon*.